The River Journey uses captivating   and compelling truths to illustrate what it means to serve the Captain wholeheartedly. Tara and Robin have an amazing way of using humorous, everyday situations to convey powerful life lessons. Stories of a sock prayer ministry, a stinkin' onion and a bread aisle are just a few of the unexpected moments that readers will experience within this book! In these pages, Tara and Robin expose the depths of their hearts—their pain, joy, laughter and tears. Well-crafted and beautifully written, *The River Journey* is a must-read for anyone desiring to seek the Kingdom more earnestly.

—Brooke Finkbiner
United Echo Worship

William Henley wrote a poem entitled "Invictus" in which he declares, "I am the master of my fate, I am the captain of my soul." A poetic rebuttal was written by Dorothea Day entitled, "My Captain." This book by Tara Hartley and Robin Holman Loy is a prosaic rebuttal to Mr. Henley. The figure of Christ as the Captain is central to Dorothea Day's poem and Tara and Robin's stories.

This book is a witness of two people who experience the pains of some bad decisions of life in a broken world and God's grace. Rivers, babies, careers and broken dreams and hope renewed with the right captain are the heart of these life stories.

I struggled a bit with the parable at the beginning, but I read the book twice and the difficulties were resolved.

They say the proof of the pudding is in the tasting, but a revision of that says the proof of the pudding is in the aftertaste.

Read this testimony by two pilgrims, read it twice and savor the aftertaste.

—N. Jefferson Brewster
Youth Pastor

Having created a parable that mirrors our journey as followers of Jesus, Robin and Tara invite us to join that journey. With frankness and honesty, they share their own journeys so that we might also walk along. As readers listen to Robin and Tara, they can find themselves and Jesus on their own journeys. It is very clear that being a Jesus follower is not about keeping a set of rules and attending worship on Sunday. Rather it is that daily, moment-by-moment, living conversation and yielding to God's love for us. The journey is about the reality of our own willful selves and the grace that God always stands ready to give. Robin and Tara have not written another "feel good" Christian book. Nor have they written a "feel bad" book. Rather, this is a book full of the reality of life and God's love and grace.

As a retired pastor, I would highly recommend this book to be used for one's own journey or in a discipling relationship with another person.

—Rev. Patricia Woolever
Retired Pastor and Retired District Superintendent
Susquehanna Conference of the United Methodist Church

Tara and Robin captivate the reader with a modern-day parable. As you read the testimonies, life strategies and tools, the parable will draw you back to a green trodden hill, the Captain's net-mending quarters and the search for gold nuggets. From the visualizations and metaphors in the parable to the signposts along the way, these ladies drop truths that we can all learn.

—Gwen Rumberger
Second Grade Teacher and Life Coach

Inspirational. Encouraging. I could not put this book down until the end. It is beautifully written. Each chapter of the book can be applied to my own journey as I aspire to see through life's challenges with Jesus as my Captain. It gave me hope and encouragement. I feel blessed to have read it. Thank you to both Tara and Robin for listening to God's voice and putting themselves out there. A true testimony that will bless many!

—Lucille Beaver

The River Journey is a beautifully written book about the journey of life. From the parable at the beginning we are drawn into the lessons that can be learned. Tara and Robin use Scripture and candidly share their life experiences to show the need for Jesus to be the Captain and the Holy Spirit to be the Navigator of our lives. Jesus wants to reveal Himself to us at all times, even in our rebellion. As Tara and Robin remind us, God peels away our stinkin' onion layers so we finally come to a point of rejoicing in any situation. That is truly real gold! If you want to develop a deeper relationship with Jesus and want Him to be your Captain, *The River Journey* is a book you will want to read.

—Deb Roush
Certified Lay Minister

My journey with Robin began when I returned from a short-term missions trip to Rwanda in 1994 and 1995 and her family involvement in that special ministry. My journey with Tara began when she and her family joined Snyder's Church in 2013, where I have now had the high honor and privilege of being their pastor since my retirement fifteen years ago.

Our mission at Snyder's Church is that "everything we do at Snyder's is about JESUS!" Both Robin and Tara represent what total commitment to Jesus is all about. After John the Baptist had been put in prison, Jesus began preaching throughout the area of the Sea of Galilee to proclaim the "the time has come...the kingdom of God has come near. Repent and believe the good news" (Mark 1:15 NIV).

If every Christian and those seeking to follow "the Way" would read the parable of *The River Journey* and then be blessed and encouraged by the R's [*Reveal, Recognize, Rebel, Refocus, Rebuild, Renew, Remember, Rejoice*] as I have been so deeply humbled, then the mission of "everything is about Jesus" and doing the will of God who sent Him would have its effects not only on our lives but also upon our dealings with everything else.

This book *The River Journey* is one that every Christian should read, purchase additional copies of and share with others. We are on this journey to serve the Lord in all ways *together*! The ministry that Tara and Robin lead—Nekoda Unlimited—is living testimony to their faith and desire to share that with others. We are indeed blessed to have the commitment of these faithful followers of Jesus. The last command of Jesus in Matthew 28:19 tells us to "go and make disciples"! Let it be so!

—Bill Pipp
Lead Pastor, Snyder's Church

What a blessing! I loved the parable with the girl and the Captain. You could really sense the presence of the Captain and the love, strength and protection that was being conveyed. I loved the way the authors' journeys were intertwined with the parable and I, as the reader, traveled with them, was aware of their struggles. The power of the Word is so relevant to everything that the readers experience as they read through the pages. Tara and Robin's stories are real, and through them we see an all-patient and providing God. I am thankful for the experience.

—Jeanette Laird
Surry, UK

The River Journey is an inspiring adventure. As Tara and Robin allow their Captain to guide them through their river journey, we also need to be aware of the strong waves that hit us and throw us off course, the

course that our Navigation Guide has us on. Where is God guiding you?
—Stephanie Freyermuth
Owner, Guardian Angel Bookstore

Beautifully and powerfully written, *The River Journey* dives deep into the crevices of heart and soul, taking the reader on an extraordinary pilgrimage. Demanding inner reflection and decisive action, Tara and Robin's authenticity and stunning vulnerability have sculpted a worthy and necessary read in the age of shocking irreverence and tolerance devoid of holiness. Thank you, Tara and Robin, for your obedience to the Captain of our souls.
—Rebecca Phillips
Writer

Foreword by Rev. James "Putter" Cox

The River Journey

Navigating the Way with Jesus

TARA HARTLEY & ROBIN HOLMAN LOY

Paperback ISBN 978-1-945169-53-3
eBook ISBN 978-1-945169-54-0

Published by
Mercy & Moxie
an imprint of
Orison Publishers, Inc.
PO Box 188, Grantham, PA 17027
www.OrisonPublishers.com

This book is dedicated to Jesus, our Captain.
We are honored to serve as He directs.
We commit this writing to you, our friends,
known and unknown,
who are ready to move forward on life's journey.

He came to his own people,
But they didn't want him.
But whoever did want him,
who believed he was who he claimed
and would do what he said,
He made to be their true selves,
their child-of-God selves.

John 1:11-12

Contents

Foreword

I don't read many Christian life books. I prefer discussions of biblical/theological issues. This book surprised me.

I was immediately drawn in by the initial Bunyanesque allegory, which reminded me even more of C.S. Lewis's wonderful (and very dense) *The Pilgrim's Regress*. It provides a great setup and is threaded well through the explanation and examples that follow.

The recurring theme is separating the wheat from the chaff in our daily lives—or, to use the authors' analogy, to seek after gold and not pyrite ("fool's gold"). The approach is theological, practical and personal. Biblical principles are elucidated using key passages rather than a barrage of proof texts, followed by explanation of how these principles can work out in our daily lives. It is further brought to life by the authors' personal examples, drawn from their very different experiences. It is quite effective!

So, enjoy the surprise! This is a worthwhile read.

—Rev. James "Putter" Cox
Pastor Emeritus, Hamilton Bible Fellowship
Protestant Chaplain, Colgate University, retired

Acknowledgments

Our journey would not be complete without our husbands and life partners, Mike and Ted, who have weathered the storms of life with us and celebrated countless joys along the way.

We are thankful for God's gifts to us of our precious children, who constantly provide us with love, support, entertainment and life material: Wilson, Caroline and Gunnar, and Sarah, Rachael, Sam, Andy, Jenn and Bryan.

We are grateful for the insight and expertise of Nicole Ensign and Sarah Loy, and we are indebted to our close friends Lori and John McClellan. Elaine and Dick Phillips, our Nekoda Unlimited team, our prayer warriors and our church families have been our constant source of loving support.

We give to God all glory and honor!

Introduction

Where We Stand

God created the universe, the world and all of its wonders. Whether we acknowledge this fact or not, we all are created by God. We are knit together by Him in our mothers' wombs as unique beings. The One who made us loves us. He has plans for us—plans to prosper us and not to harm us. (See Jeremiah 1:5, 29:11.)

Some of us know God (our Creator, our everlasting Father, our Provider, our Healer and our Peace) and believe in Him. Some of us do not. Some of us know Jesus as the Son of God and our Shepherd and believe in Him as our way to eternal living. Some of us do not. Some of us know and believe that the Holy Spirit is the abiding Presence who guides and encourages us. Some of us do not. We believe that God, Jesus and the Holy Spirit make up the Trinity—three in one.

Belief—or unbelief—does not change who God is or what He does.

This book was written by two of us who know God as our way, Jesus as our Captain, and the Holy Spirit as our Navigator—simply said but difficult to explain. We are vessels for Jesus. We have no special training or pedigree to give us more insight than you have. We merely have a story to tell for those who feel something is missing or who may be asleep. This book is also for those who are hopeless or who feel unworthy or who have lost their way.

Our purpose in writing this book is to encourage you to have a deeper relationship with Jesus. Our experience has led us to the conclusion that all of us are on a "river journey." In this metaphor, the river represents life. Your journey through life will not be like our journeys, but there will be similarities. We all start our journey at birth in a boat. Our boats travel within God's river. God allows us to make choices that take us off course; we all have the choice to stay close to God or explore elsewhere.

By sharing our stories, we hope to help you evaluate where you are on your river journey. Our goal is to help you recognize Jesus as your lifeline and Captain and the Holy Spirit as your guide and Navigator. We do not claim to know everything, for we know that we do not know much. But what we do know is that God loves you and us beyond our wildest imaginations! We are cherished. He wants us to know and believe in Him because He is our greatest cheerleader, our most faithful partner and our toughest taskmaster.

So, come join us on a journey with Jesus—a journey that will:

Reveal Him to us.

Allow us to *recognize* our need for Him.

Tune us in to how we *rebel* against Him.

Refocus our hearts on Him.

Rebuild what is broken in us, which threatens to sink us.

Renew a right spirit within us.

Help us *remember* that He meets us in this moment.

And teach us to *rejoice* in the Lord always.

I
The River Journey

Navigating the Way with Jesus: A Parable

My scream echoes in the silence. My body is almost totally encased in a slimy bog of decayed undergrowth. I'm not sure how much longer I can keep my nose and eyes above the surface of the swamp. The more I struggle, the faster I slip down deeper into my demise. The island landscape mocks me. The lure of the unknown had drawn me further inland; I had felt it calling to me, calling me away from the river. Why did I follow?

Back in the beginning…

I cannot remember a time when I was not in the boat or involved with the river. My earliest memories take me back to life safely inside the boat floating on the water. My Captain was ever present on board the boat and all my comforts were provided. Others lived in the boat as well, and I remember laughing and playing with them. At that time, I didn't have many responsibilities and spent most of my time daydreaming and leaning over the side to gaze through the water at shimmering gold nuggets.

As I grew older, my daydreams were interrupted by watching the Captain as He worked and oversaw the daily tasks performed on the boat. He was fascinating! Extreme fluidity made His intense work seem effortless as He balanced three main tasks. He directed the boat, supervised the work associated with the nets, and selected and directed the gold gatherers. Somehow, He did all of this simultaneously! My attention was captured not only by His personal ability to complete tasks but also by how He made each person on the boat feel. It was easy to see that the workers were confident when challenged, capable while confronted and courageous during chaos. Those at rest were peaceful. Everyone held an inner joy that reverberated throughout the boat. Unreserved devotion to the Captain was obvious.

While watching the Captain, I was most impressed by how He managed the details of His main tasks. When directing our way, the Captain chose the course of our boat and relayed those plans to the Navigator. He knew the river waters well and charted our path steadily around many islands as well as snares, such as sandbars and rocks. He would inventory our supplies and determine which islands we would dock at and for how long. He also kept record of who went ashore and who remained safely on the boat.

When supervising the work associated with the nets, everything required sorting. Nets were used everywhere on the boat and came in all sizes and strengths for many different functions. Small nets were used for gathering gold and distributing food. Medium and large nets were used for fishing and holding large supplies. There were also mysterious extralarge nets. I wasn't sure what those were used for because the Captain always instructed the workers to take the extralarge nets to the other side of the boat where only a few people were invited. While I manned my station on the boat, I idly watched how great care was taken with all the nets to ensure that there were no holes, rips or unraveling and that all were kept in good working order.

His gold-gathering tasks were most intriguing to me, especially as I grew older. I never knew how each mission would unfold. The basics of gold gathering encompassed the selection of different people to go out into the water on a mission to collect specific gold pieces. How He determined which gold was meant for a specific person at a certain spot in the river, I'll never know. I mean, there was so much gold! No matter where I looked, gold flickered in the river. One important point about gold-gathering we all learned was to select only the gold indicated for the mission and not to bring back more or less than authorized. There was no magic age for being selected as a gold gatherer, as far as I could surmise. Whether someone was young or old, gold gathering was for anyone whom the Captain called.

I was extremely curious about gold gathering. One thing I noticed was that the Captain would send people into the river in all kinds of weather and varying river depths! Sometimes the sun shimmered on the shallow water so brightly that it was hard to distinguish the sparkling rays on the top from the sparkling nuggets underneath. These were the easiest gold-gathering missions. At other times, the river was so deep I would catch only a glimpse of the treasure in the depths. These forays were more challenging and took more time.

The worst was when He would send gatherers into a chaotic storm. I never understood what He was thinking! Wasn't the gold all the same? Wouldn't it be better to grab all we could in the shallows and sunshine and avoid sending anyone into the water on stormy nights? This is where my first disagreement with the Captain evolved in my head. This danger felt unnecessary and avoidable. Storms were very intimidating; I was glad to stay in the shelter of the boat where everything was in my control. I would huddle under my blanket while the water thrashed against the boat as we rocked and pitched. "Please let my gold-gathering day be full of sunshine and shallow water!" I prayed. As the team assembled, wind and rain whipped at their clothes and hair. I remember how shocked I was when I braved a peek at the faces of the group from my secure station on the boat. Unbelievable! Each newly and carefully chosen gatherer looked determined and confident in the face of such a terrible storm!

Time continued to pass, and I entered my latter teen years. I had yet to be selected to gather gold, and, frankly, it was no longer important to me. The selection method I observed over the years was full of discrepancies. There seemed to be no rhyme or reason to it, and I couldn't follow the Captain's logic. I was just as capable as others who were chosen—probably more so. However, I certainly didn't want to draw attention to myself and get picked to go out in one of those awful storms. I felt it best to enjoy life on the boat away from the center of activity, staying busy by doing the things I enjoyed.

I tried to stay content within my life on the boat, but to tell the truth, I wasn't. I did spend most of my days imagining what it would be like to hold a piece of gold in my hand. I had not yet been allowed off the boat when we docked and desperately ached to feel the sand beneath my toes. I listened enviously to the stories of the ones who were allowed off the boat. My imagination created scenarios—from what it felt like to stand on dry land, to hauling in nets full of giant nuggets, to hearing the stories told of my bounty. Oh! The visions my mind created! If I were allowed to gather gold from the shoreline of the river, what sweet success would it hold for me?

I am startled as I catch the first glimpse of an island and its beauty. It is straight out of my fantasy! As we approach, I can see right away that it is different than other islands where we previously docked. The white-sand beach and the lush green vegetation further inland spellbind me. The chorus of tropical birds is a symphony to my ears! I also see hills on this island. Some are big and some are small, but there is definitely a rolling landscape. As we pull closer to the dock, I am so absorbed by every new color and sound that I almost don't hear the Captain call my name.

"Yes?" I answer.

"You may go ashore with us today," says the Captain. "Please be ready with your essentials when we are secured."

At first I am shocked, but then I am overjoyed and elated! He called my name! How long will we be staying? I wonder. Do I have any type of assignment? Is this the island where I will gather gold? Should I take a net? What size? Where is my backpack with my essentials? I need my manual, my water bottle and my multi-tool. It was the most

4

basic rule on the boat never to leave without these items. The manual is a bit bulky but critical if I come up against a question on shore to which I don't know the answer. That seems unlikely, but I don't want to delay my departure by not following protocol. The water bottle fulfills a more fundamental need, but it is obviously useless if left empty. Finally, my multi-tool—now this is a handy item! It is made of two pieces of wood attached to each other perpendicularly. Each end is fashioned into a toolhead that performs different functions. It takes up as much space as my manual, but all in all, my backpack is still light. My mind races! I want to remember every detail about my time on shore.

As we dock and the boat is secured, the Captain stands near the gangway watching passengers disembark as well as board. As I walk past Him, I suddenly realize I have never been this close to Him before. It catches me off guard that He seems closer to normal size than to the image of Him I hold in my mind. I should stop and converse with Him about why He chose me to go ashore or at least ask if I have a specific task to accomplish, but I am too eager to feel the sand between my toes.

I pause at the end of the gangway, about to take my first step onto the island. I call a quick question back over my shoulder. "Captain? What's the name of this island?"

"It is the Isle of Eye. Please stay close."

Stay close? What does He mean by that? My toes burrow into the sand as I ponder His words; I decide that He probably means that I should stay close enough to hear Him. I don't think I have to actually stay on the beach because He never gave me a particular job. The island seems nice here, but there's not much to do but help Him mend the nets, and I would rather explore. It looks to me like there are plenty of other people who could help Him, anyway.

Besides, this is a beautiful paradise! I want to explore a bit just to see what the island has to offer. I'll stay within earshot, I think. As I approach the tree line, the sense that maybe I should not venture further rises up. It is a small, warm feeling that makes me pivot and cock my head. Maybe I should just tell Him that I am going to check things out for a while so He knows where I am in case He needs me.

I look over at the Captain and see He is busy with a mess of nets. Of course, if He didn't throw the nets out at the height of a storm, they wouldn't become so tangled. I know the nets can be used in all kinds of weather in water or on dry land, but why can't He wait for clear, calm and peaceful moments before He acts? He creates His own tangles because He uses them when He shouldn't! Where is everyone, anyway? I was so busy thinking about leaving the beach that I never noticed where anyone else was going. Well, given the choice between working and exploring, I guess they also chose the more enjoyable and exciting option.

I turn away from the beach and survey my surroundings. I can see numerous paths leading into the woods. Although I still feel a bit of hesitation, I decide to follow a path for a short while. I can always get back to the boat after I explore. The Captain won't even miss me. Besides, He isn't looking for anyone right now! I wheel around and choose a path. At its entrance into the trees, there is a gnome-sized signpost with exquisite gold lettering. It reads GE3. I tilt my head, contemplating the meaning. It seems like a path number for a map I've seen before, but I can't quite remember the details. I shrug and move on.

The moment I step under the first tree, I can feel the coolness of the path. It is refreshing. Birds are singing and tree frogs are chirping. It is a pleasant rolling path, and all I can think about is what adventures lie ahead. After a few minutes of walking, the path inclines upward. I stop and turn. Can I still see the beach? I can't really, but I can see where I entered the woods, so I convince myself that I am still close enough to hear Him shout.

As I turn back to the path and look ahead, my eyes catch the gleam of something off to the side of the path. I rush over to see what it is. Wow! It's a large nugget of gold! I can't believe I found one so easily and without the need to dive into the river! I am sure the Captain will be pleased and surprised. What will all the others say about my treasure? I place it in my backpack and look further down the path. I had no idea the island had treasure like this. The voice of sweet success rings in my ears. Without hesitation, I charge onward in search of more gold.

The path looks like it continues upward. When I get to the top, I will probably be able to see the beach and maybe the rest of the island. As I hike onward, I realize I am hungry. I never thought to pack any food, but of course I didn't think I was going this far for this long. How long has it been? I am startled to realize that I have no idea how long I have been hiking. I have been so focused on looking for gold and getting to the top that I haven't even stopped to see where I am or what time it is.

I am suddenly not only hungry but very thirsty. In my excitement to get off the boat, I forgot to fill my water bottle. I shake my head in disbelief at my oversight. I look up the pathway and glimpse some sunshine just ahead. I also can make out another small signpost with PS107 engraved on it. It must be a bearing of some kind or a marker for the path, I puzzle. With renewed energy, I push myself onward.

I think I'm right; I'm at the top of the hill. But my excitement turns to disappointment when I realize I am not high enough to see the beach. I can't even see the boat. Fortunately, way in the distance, I catch the sparkle of the sun on the water. At least I can see how to get back.

I focus on what's right in front of me. It appears that others have been here before me because I see the remnants of a campfire and a sign that says, "Relax—you deserve it." No truer words have ever been spoken, I say to myself. I do deserve a rest! I've been hiking for a while, and I need some downtime with food and liquid refreshment. Upon further inspection, I see what appears to be a watering hole with lots of small gold nuggets sparkling throughout the shallow water. Eureka! I also see another signpost beside it engraved with JN4. Once again, I'm flummoxed. What does that mean? Maybe it is a marker for watering holes.

There are footprints leading up to the water, signaling that others have been here, too. Not seeing any skeletons or evidence that the water is unsafe, I lean down and fill my water bottle. While taking large gulps of water, my eyes are fixated on the numerous gold nuggets strewn throughout the shallow water. With renewed strength, I wade into the water and rapidly collect as many as I can, stuffing the treasure into my backpack. I am excited to find so much gold. Satisfied, I sit down to contemplate my next move.

I am still very hungry. A fleeting thought enters my mind, urging me to go back down the hill and get on the boat. Our boat always had enough food, water and shelter. As I lean back against a tree trunk, I have another momentary thought of the Captain and His directive to "stay close." But then I see the sign right in front of me: "relax—you deserve it"! I close my eyes, thinking that I'll just stay here for a bit and rest. Then I can find some food.

I wake with a start. How long have I been dozing? I am freezing. How can that be? It was a perfect temperature when I closed my eyes. Then I remember the campfire. It never dawned on me that I would need a fire to keep warm. My concern is mounting. Now I am not only hungry, but also cold!

As I survey my surroundings, I know that I need to take care of myself. I also know there is no food in this precise location. The path seems a bit less defined than earlier in my journey, and little sunshine is filtering through the vegetation. However, there is another one of those little signposts engraved with JN6. Maybe J isn't the coordinate for watering holes but a path designation, as I thought before. If I had the map, I might be able to figure it out. Again, something seems familiar. Could it be in my manual? However, right now I don't have time to sit and page through that bulky book.

I've got to go. I can't stay here and freeze. I need to get warm! Besides, there is no food. I need to get moving and find some food. It never occurs to me to go back to the boat. I don't even think about the Captain in my quest to comfort myself.

I start towards the path leading down the hill. There is a dense tree canopy overhead, blocking out much of the sun. As I pick my way down the hill, I soon discover that it is also extremely foggy. I keep tripping over the signposts that litter the path. I can't see them through the darkness and fog, but thankfully I catch myself each time. At one point, I think I see shadows of others on the path ahead of me. My steps quicken, trying to catch up to them. I would feel better if I were with someone else on this path.

The path winds through an S-turn, and I have to exert myself to make it around and up the hill. As I put my head down, digging deep for strength to continue, I notice it is getting lighter and glimpse another gold nugget peeking at me from under a rock. My spirits lift as I scoop it up and drop it into my backpack. As I swing the backpack up onto my shoulder, I notice that it is getting heavy. I struggle to get it adjusted on my shoulder. With thoughts of "I can do this," I persevere onward.

Suddenly, I come out of the fog into a clearing. I've made it to the top of a bigger hill where many paths converge. In the center of the convergence is a huge circle. It looks like the circle has been well worn, as if people have been walking around and around within the circle. Each path off the circle leads in a different direction. Some appear to be more traveled. I wonder why?

I stop in the circle to get my bearings. I remember on the boat we were headed north, I think. When I entered the vegetation after leaving the camping spot, I was heading east. How does that help? Assuming the path I was on did not change direction, if I go left I'll be heading north, parallel to the river. However, it appears that going left is not the usual path people take. The footsteps are all headed to the right, which is counterclockwise.

I pause and will myself to think logically about my options. As I stand there contemplating my situation, I am distracted by a vague, persistent hum that I can hear but cannot identify. At first it just seems like annoying background noise, but it continues like a pesky mosquito. I try to ignore it so I can concentrate and figure out my dilemma. Which way to go?

As I walk to the right, the way of the many footsteps, there are so many paths. I move further into the circle to get a better vantage point. From here I can see, in the distance, steeples and countless buildings. There is even one that seems to radiate light. The sun reflecting off what looks like milky marble stones creates a halo effect around the imposing architectural wonder. What's the sign say on the next building? I squint to try to make out the letters. "MM&I"—maybe they are university buildings or an institute of some sort? If I look really hard, I can see teeny tiny figures moving in and out of the buildings. Some are holding things and walking towards others who receive the things. After the exchange, the ones receiving the things sit down. As far as my eyes can see, there are lots of people sitting and only a few moving.

I continue around the circle, marveling at the number of paths. I pause and notice that I am straight across from the path I used to enter into the circle, I think. When I turn my back on that path, I presume I am again looking towards the east. I see a sign pointing to a magnificent tower. It states, "Self-reverence, Self-knowledge, Self-fulfillment."

What a curious sign! Near the sign are more of the gnomelike sign-posts with golden engraved letters and numbers. One says 1C1533, and further down the path, another signpost reads EC1; the signposts continue with JA316, JA4, JA5, GA520, LK1425.... My mind searches for their meaning, but I can't discern anything because that annoying buzz is getting louder.

I peruse the tower. The more I stare, the more I can see. It stretch-es towards the sky and has many golden turrets, colorful levels, stone terraces and balconies with hanging vines. I can see people moving past large plate-glass windows. Some seem to be relaxing on the ter-races and balconies with fancy drinks. Others seem to be in a hurry. Still others are climbing ladders to get to the next levels. It seems like a beehive of activity. As I squint to get a better look, I can see a person at the top of a turret yelling at me. What is he saying? "Help?" That's odd. I struggle to hear his words, but that annoying buzz has turned into an awful din and drowns out the sound. In short order, several people appear beside the man and pull him back from the turret. I feel disconcerted, like I should have helped him; but realistically, what could I have done?

The good thing is that if there are people in the tower, they must have food and water. Upon closer scrutiny, I see there is a moat around the tower. How did the people get in there? There doesn't seem to be any entranceway. Of course, I can't see the whole thing. Maybe the entrance is around back.

As I continue around the circle on the hilltop to survey my op-tions, I look to the paths presumably going towards the north. It appears that there are more rolling hills in that direction. I notice a river in the distance and what appear to be boats with people in them. When I see the boats, my heart warms and I become hopeful. Maybe they are good people like the ones I know on the boat with the Captain. Oh! I have not thought about the Captain in a long time. Maybe I should turn around and go back the way I came. I know I was taken care of when I was with Him. But as I turn, I realize that I don't know which path I used to come into the circle anymore. I am disoriented. With a start, I realize that I have lost my way. For the first time, I'm shaken.

I continue to walk around the circle because I don't know what else to do. I do know that my backpack filled with gold is weighing me down and starting to hurt my back. A signpost fleetingly catches my attention—MT620. But I can't take this backpack digging into my shoulders any longer. I drop it onto the path and sift through the contents, realizing that I have other stuff in there that I don't need. I throw aside the bulky, heavy manual that I got on the boat, as well as the multi-tool. Neither of them has been useful yet; I doubt they will be. Besides, it is much more important to get the gold back to the boat, so I can show everyone what and how much I gathered. I throw the extraneous stuff by the side of the path near a signpost reading 2TI315. After I rearrange the gold nuggets, I swing the backpack onto my shoulders and position it more comfortably on my back. That's better! It is still pretty heavy, though.

At this point, it seems like I have circled the whole way around the hilltop, but I continue to see new paths that lead to unknown places. I am starting to worry. The signposts are everywhere on the paths, but I don't even bother trying to figure out what they mean. I am far more concerned about my own state. I am increasingly hungry, thirsty and tired. I can't believe I forgot to refill my water bottle when I left the watering hole. I start to despair. Walking around the circle trying to decide which path to take has totally confused me and is sapping my strength. It seems like if I don't just pick a path, I'll be stuck in this circle forever.

I can't help but think that if I could talk with someone, he or she could fill me in on what is going on and help me get to the right path. But everyone I see is far away; those people look like they are too involved in what they are doing to notice me. As a matter of fact, no one has even noticed that I am stuck in this circle on a hilltop. If they would but look up and notice, they could help me find my way. But what "way" am I looking for? Where do I want to go? What is the meaning of all these signposts? I am so confused.

Suddenly, I hear a great commotion coming towards the circle from one of the paths. As the seconds tick by, the noise gets louder and louder, like a thundering herd of wild horses. The deafening sound shakes the ground, and I realize I had better run—and run quickly. So

I do, veering off the circle and onto a random path that appears to lead towards the distant river I saw that had boats. I pause, panting heavily, and cover my ears. The sound is so loud that my head throbs and I have to close my eyes. Finally, the sound diminishes, and I am able to open my eyes; but all I can see is dust and fast-moving shadows. My mind desperately wants to know what is happening in the circle. For a split second, I am tempted to step back into the dust and see what all the commotion is about, but my gut warns me that is a bad choice. I sense that I got out of the circle just in the nick of time. I turn away and start down the path. A great wave of exhaustion comes over me, and I stop by a signpost that reads MT1128.

I sit down limply on a stump beside the signpost. I can't even move on. I start to cry, sobs shaking my shoulders. Where am I? What am I doing? I am lost on this God-forsaken island. What should I do? Where should I go? I can't ask anyone for advice because no one is around. No one can help me, anyway. I certainly can't seem to help myself. At that moment, I realize I have never before been this hungry, thirsty or lonely. I am miserable! As my sobs subside, I dig deep inside for courage to continue down this path.

Immediately I notice that I am walking downhill. The path winds briefly through colorful flowers. Their beauty encourages me. As I slowly walk downward, the path takes a turn into a heavily vegetated forest. I hear sounds that I don't recognize and glimpse things moving that frighten me. I stop. Should I turn around? No. That just leads back to the circle where the chaos is. Besides, I was just going around and around in that circle with nothing good happening, anyway. I don't know if the dust has settled yet, either. It could be that the herd is still blocking the way.

I need to go forward. I feel that urging in my core. I'm guessing the river is ahead. "I can make it," I tell myself. I move more quickly, not caring that I am trampling through increasingly sloppy mud, decayed vegetation and muck. The air is becoming much cooler, and moisture begins seeping through my shirt. The dampness makes me shiver. I force myself to totally focus on the path ahead and ignore the weird sounds and the creepy feeling that starts traveling up my spine. Panic tries to set in, but I clamp down on my emotions, willing myself to remain focused on one step at a time. Abruptly, one foot becomes immobile—and then the other. I freeze; my panic overwhelms me. I am stuck and sinking!

Hysterical, I attempt to back up, but my feet are cemented in the muck that is pulling me down. I fight to pull each foot out, but neither budges. I twist, looking for something to grab—a branch or vine—but I can't reach anything. The more I struggle, the deeper I sink. *What is happening?* My mind recoils in terror; I scream. The forest becomes totally quiet. There is no sound but the beating of my heart. As the mud moves surprisingly quickly up my torso, I suddenly know deep down in my soul that I am going to sink into this bog. No one will know what happened; I simply will vanish without a trace. I can't do anything. There are no fixes here, and no one is going to rescue me. I am going to die!

My scream echoes in the silence. My body is almost totally encased in this slimy bog of decayed undergrowth. I'm not sure how much longer I can keep my nose and eyes above the surface. The more I struggle, the faster I slip down deeper into my demise. The annoying buzz that plagued me on this tragic journey has morphed into mocking laughter.

As the putrid slime closes over my face and I fade from consciousness, a last thought fills my mind: "Help me, my Captain…."

A hand reaches through the dark and pulls me into the light.

I am dragged up onto stable ground. Coughing, choking, desperate for breath, I flounder, expelling the sludge and putrid water from my body. Everything is blurry, and I'm losing consciousness. What happened? Am I dreaming? Who saved me?

I realize with a fuzzy awareness that someone is carrying me. I can feel the steady, gentle gait of His footsteps. I am alive! The tree canopy shelters me from the sun, and I have a fleeting memory of the beach, the river and my boat. My muddy, slimy hair is plastered to my face, and a wretched taste fills my mouth. I have no strength to lift my head, which is dangling over an arm of steel. I drift out of awareness and back into an abyss of unconsciousness.

Slowly, my senses come back to life. The first thing I recognize is a sound. The lapping of water at the river's shoreline is gently trying to pull me awake. The sound is peaceful and calm. I can feel that I am lying stretched out on something hard as I attempt to open my eyes. My eyelids flutter, and the sun crashes through. I wince from the sting. The sand I once thought felt like velvet is now gritty and scratchy against my skin. I am filthy. My own stench makes me gag, and I spit grime from my mouth. I am embarrassed as well as plain disgusted. I realize that I'm crying; all I want is to go home. I want to be in my comfortable shelter on the boat, away from everyone. Gone is the explorer and confident treasure seeker. I am humiliated, scared and painfully aware of my disheveled state. Will I be allowed back on the boat? I'm so ashamed.

"Please stay close" keeps echoing in my mind. Why did I refuse to listen?

With a great deal of effort, I pull myself off the hard-packed sand and crawl into the river to rid myself of the smelly yuck. Driving me forward is the thought of collapsing into my station on the boat, never to emerge again. Hopefully I'll be able to sneak back to my quarters unnoticed. If I can just cross the gangplank and get through the gate quietly without attracting attention, I'll be okay.

Far from clean but at least without sludge hanging from me, I dash up the gangplank to the gate. The gate is latched; I can't get in without knocking. Why is everything so hard?! I risk being seen in this state if I knock, but what other choice do I have? If I stay out here on the gangplank, I'll surely be discovered. I attempt the softest of taps on the gate, and blessedly it swings open. Midway through the gate opening, my eyes instantly lock with the Captain's. Even across the span of the boat, His eyes speak volumes to me while His hands remain on the helm.

What do His eyes hold? Is it contempt? Is it disappointment? Confusion startles me because His gaze doesn't feel that way. I certainly have a boatload of feelings of contempt and disappointment towards myself, but the Captain's eyes do not hold those judgments. His eyes are saying something different. What is it?

I break eye contact and turn away. I scurry to my station, only to vomit from my anxiety. How many people just saw me? My obvious disobedient behavior is spelled out in the state of my clothes and the reek of my person. I must get clean! But I can't pass by these people again! I should have gone straight to the washroom. How dumb am I? I can't go out again—I won't. I'll just wait in my quarters until dark, when I can sneak back to the washroom. My only option is to curl up on the floor; there is no way I'm crawling into my bed like this.

It is well into the night when I feel a gentle hand on my shoulder. I must have fallen asleep. It is the Captain, and I recoil. No one should touch me; I'm so dirty. He can see my distress and simply says, "Come, follow Me. I have everything you need."

With head low in defeated submission, I follow Him. The night seems extra black as we cross the deck to the washroom. He probably wants me clean so I don't infect the others on the boat or make them sick by my stench. How does He stand to be so close to me? At least, that's what I think as I scrub my body and hair with the soap He provided. Why else would He help me?

When I emerge from the washroom in the clean clothes He brought, I am startled to see Him still waiting. He quietly asks me for my stained clothing. Will this shame never end? As I hand them over to Him, I am acutely aware of how there would be no stained clothes had I obeyed His simple request.

Through the black night we silently walk back to my quarters. I desperately want to tell Him how sorry I am that I disobeyed. I want to say how sorry I am for bringing that yuck onto His boat and, most of all, how thankful I am that He saved me. But I say nothing because I am so afraid and ashamed that I can't even lift my head. Hot tears pour down my face, dripping down onto my feet. Then He gently raises my chin with His fingers and sweetly says, "I'm so glad you are home. Please rest until I come for you."

Time holds no concept for me as my body heals and my bruises fade. At first, I can barely move off my cot because my muscles are so sore from my futile fight in the bog. The external bruises on my body are easily visible. It's ironic how a bruise can get uglier as it moves through the healing process.

Ever by my side, the Captain is my constant companion. He provides me with food and water as well as keeps my station fresh and clean. Eventually, He starts taking me on small jaunts around the deck. Most of the time we say little to each other, but He has a way of speaking without words and of knowing my limits. My muscles need to be stretched and exercised. He seems in tune with what overwhelms my growing confidence, and it is in those times that He pulls me close.

As time passes, He allows me to observe Him as He performs His duties on the boat. I hover in the background as He talks with the Navigator about charting our upcoming course on the river. I accompany Him as He instructs the net workers on their tasks for the day. When it comes time for Him to choose His gold gatherers, I often ask to remain at my station. Gathering gold or having anything to do with gold is painful to me now. It is a constant reminder of something I used to measure as success, but now it produces only humiliation. I feel flawed by my ambition to gather gold on my own, and I am more than aware that it almost cost me my life.

One day, while on a walk around the upper deck, I ask the Captain which job on the boat is His favorite. He surprises me when He says, "I like the care of the extralarge nets." I'd forgotten about those big nets. They are kept on the opposite side of the boat from my station, far from my view. Here, from our position on the upper deck, though, I can see all sorts of activity that I never knew about. I can see new nets being made as well as snarled and tangled nets being repaired. Looking down, I see a net that is all twisted into a ball and covered with muck. I ask the Captain if the tangles can be fixed or if the net just needs to be thrown away. He assures me that the nets can be put back together.

He explains that it takes time to untangle them because these nets cannot be separated or cut. Each part of the net is very important and cannot be discarded. He compares an extralarge, tangled net with a person who has lost his or her way.

"Sometimes," He explains, "the remedy a person needs isn't obvious. We can see the big knot but not the path that the ropes must take to smooth the snarl. The same thing happens with people. They get stuck in a twisted web that they are aware of but just can't fix alone."

I wonder to myself if He is talking about me or someone else. His patient teachings coupled with His gentle, compassionate ways are mending me from the inside out.

I am taking a walk by myself in view of the Captain when the happy, tinkling sound of a wind chime directs my attention to the edge of the boat. As I peek over the side, I catch a glimpse of gold! Instantly, memories of dark, mucky water filling my ears and throat threaten to overwhelm me. I remember where I once was. I feel the darkness closing in on me again. Pulse racing, I hurry back to my shelter. How could I forget? How could I let my guard down enough to even lean over the rail of the boat? I want to stay on the boat. I do not want to get off the boat ever again.

Ever faithful, patient and forgiving, the Captain understands my trepidation. He draws me to the present with reminders of what I have learned since my island horror. He always speaks of my time on the island as a learning process and has never condemned me for my errors. He openly speaks to me about my choices on the island and encourages me to move past the pain. He says the past is not to be removed or forgotten but is to be used as a net of sorts to help someone else in some way in the future. I do not fully understand what that means. How are my trials and tribulations a net?

Steadily I grow in strength and confidence, and my bond with the Captain becomes unshakable. We spend time walking the deck and conversing about His duties and the responsibilities on the boat. Today, as we walk back to my quarters discussing different tasks assigned to others on the boat, a question impulsively flies out of my mouth.

"Why didn't You give me a task when we were on the Isle of Eye?"

He responds, "Do you think that a task would have kept you from exploring?"

"I don't know. Maybe," I stutter.

My thoughts are quickly becoming jumbled, and my shame rises. We are suddenly at my station. In a voice just a touch above a whisper, I rush through my next questions, ones that I have been holding inside but can no longer keep from asking. "Why did You choose that horrible island for me? Why was I never chosen as a gold gatherer on the boat? Why didn't You need me before?" My silent tears slide down my face. I hate that I sound as if I am blaming Him for my actions, but I can't help it.

"Those are all very good questions, and it is very brave of you to ask," He responds gently. "First, the Isle of Eye holds as many treasures as it holds tragedies. The distinction lies in whose directions you are following on the island: your own or Mine. Second, it is critical for gold gatherers to have more love for Me than for themselves. That kind of love builds trust. Gold gatherers understand that they will not always know what is happening or why, but they do know I will never leave them or forsake them. They must trust I will keep them safe at all times. The more dangerous the mission is, the more they are called to trust and obey Me. Finally, I'll answer your last question with another question that I'll leave you to ponder. When was the first time you really needed Me? Was it on the boat you've lived on your whole life, or was it when I saved you from certain death?"

With a kiss on my forehead, the Captain goes on His way. His answers make my mind spin. His directions or my own? I always assumed the Isle of Eye was spelled like the sensory organ, but what if it was spelled with a capital *I*? That is certainly who I was following: *me*. Gold gathering's purpose was really about trust and obedience, not about the quantity of gold? Really? No wonder I have never been chosen. I am not qualified. The only one I trust and obey is myself.

When did I first really need the Captain? Sure, I watched Him day in and day out when I was young, but His responsibilities didn't really concern me. They weren't part of my daily life. My daily life centered on *I—me, myself and I*. It is with a full mind and heavy heart that I sink into my cot. The winds of change are at my door.

As the sun comes up over the horizon, the first notable transformative behavioral shift occurs. Before, I did not know He was waiting for me. Now, I awake early and wait for Him to come out of His quarters. I am not concerned about how long I wait because I am prepared. I have my new essentials bag filled with my new manual, new water bottle (filled), and my new multi-tool. His eyes sparkle when He sees me sitting at His door.

"Good morning," He declares.

"Good morning, Captain. I am ready to be put to work today. How can I help You?"

"Come and follow Me," He says with a broad smile.

Together we walk to the far side of the boat where the extralarge nets are maintained and crafted. He explains that the extralarge nets need the greatest care, as they carry the most precious cargo. I don't know what that cargo is, but it no longer matters to me. What matters is that I am not focused on myself, but on how I can help the Captain. We tour the different stations where the huge nets are repaired and created. The people called to work in the extralarge net area always start in the repair area, so that is where my learning begins.

The repair area is separated into two parts: the untangle section and the knot section. Used nets are hauled in and inspected in the repair area. After inspection, the net is sent to the untangle section. I learn that unless the net is completely untangled before patching, small tears or weaknesses can be overlooked. I thrive in the simplicity of routine and blossom as I complete each task assigned to me. I feel a sense of accomplishment and am thankful to be able to do my small part.

Each day, I learn something new. For instance, untangling an extralarge net requires patience, persistence and a certain kind of tenacity. I learn to approach each new tangled net as if it is an exquisite, beautiful, one-of-a-kind giant puzzle. My multi-tool is essential to the untangling process. It's a curious thing. When I hold it in my hands, not only is it practically useful, but it also fills my mind with thoughts of the Captain, from how much I love and trust Him to how much I rely on Him.

Sometimes it seems as if more snarls develop in the process of untangling! But at those moments, I remember that the Captain is in charge. He reminds me that many times things get worse in order for Him to make them better. He teaches that bad things do happen and that I will not always understand this process. He explains that sometimes He cannot totally reveal everything to gold gatherers because they might become distracted and tangle a net further. Eventually the mess seems to unravel smoothly, and the net moves on to the other side of the repair area: the knot section.

I come to understand that what holds any net together are special types of knots. Upon moving out of the untangling area, I need to spend time mastering the art of knot tying before I work on actual nets. Learning this skill requires me to constantly refer to my manual for guidance and directions. How did I think this was just a bulky, useless book? I can see that the more I spend time delving into the depths of the manual, the more I remember its various principles. These principles become the foundations of the knots. It is critical that all new knots stay strong when a net is loaded and put to the test.

My days are busy and flow by happily as we sail on the river. My Captain is always wherever my eyes look. It almost seems that all I have to do is picture Him, and He appears—not always at my side, but at a place where I can see Him at work. I meet many wonderful people in the repair area of the extralarge nets, but eventually it is time for me to move on in my journey.

The Captain takes me to the creating area of the extralarge nets. I must admit I am intimidated. I see people winding the rope and placing the knots in various places. I see that each net is slightly different. None are alike, but each is a masterpiece! The configuration of the knots and spaces comes from a plan of the Captain's that the workers can see in their hearts. The Captain instructs the workers and brings each masterpiece to life with rope and knots. It is hard to sit and study the plan and listen to the Captain at the same time.

As I work, I realize that when I err, the Captain sends someone else to help. I am certainly glad I am not in this alone and that He is in charge! I also realize that the net can get tangled for obvious and not-so-obvious reasons that only the Captain knows about. I remember the lessons I learned on the island and am glad He was ultimately in charge of that whole adventure. I guess that's why I learned to untangle the net first—so I could try to keep His plan and design in the forefront of my mind.

My early days in the creating area are long and slow. I study my manual constantly for direction and ask the Captain questions when I get stuck. At times, I get so angry with myself for not being able to catch on as quickly as others seem to be able to do. Why is this so hard? As I work, I notice the lady beside me is doing a great job with the Captain's net that He assigned to her. Her work seems so strong and correct. I resist the temptation to be jealous and copy what she is doing. Instead, we become friends and begin to share wisdom that the Captain has imparted to each of us. I come away from our conversations with new insights that I can't wait to share with the Captain and hopefully incorporate into my assignment.

Once I learn not to look at others' assignments but to stay focused on the one I am helping the Captain with, things start to become simpler. Each day becomes easier, and my assignments take on a new rhythm. It is with anticipation that I come to work each day! I start my day in my manual for inspiration, and my net becomes an outpouring of my heart. The placement of each knot is done with care and precision.

"Please pick up your net and your multi-tool and follow Me. I need you," the Captain calls.

"Okay, but why, Captain? I'm enjoying myself here. I'm comfortable, and I really think I'm getting the hang of net design," I respond enthusiastically.

"Well done. You excelled at untangling and knotting the nets, and your personal net design is exquisitely completed according to My plan. It is easy to see how your signature knots will fulfill a distinct need. Now I need you to put your net to work to haul precious cargo—and you are the only one who can cast it."

I cheerfully gather my net as I follow Him out of the extra-large net area. Numerous questions pop up. "What is the cargo my net will carry, Captain? Anyone can cast my net; I'll happily give it to anyone who needs it." But before another question can spill out, the Captain stops walking. We are standing at the top of the gangplank. I suddenly realize that the boat has docked and is secured at an island.

I start backing away slowly from the gate. Why are we here? I don't have to get off the boat, do I? The Captain answers my silent question.

"I need you to go ashore and cast your net. Your net is built from My plan and is designed from your heart. It can help people on this island who have had experiences similar to yours."

I don't know what to say. I know I do not want any part of exiting the boat onto this island, but He is asking me to do this. He, My Captain, my Shelter, my Provider and my Protector, is asking for my help. How do I say no?

"I don't think I can do this—I mean, I don't know that I'm strong enough to throw this net," I mumble.

"Do you think we can do it together? I can give you the strength you need to cast this extralarge net," He gently urges.

"Okay, but I don't know the way. How will I find people on the island? What if I get lost?" I hesitantly murmur.

"Do you think you can follow My lead? I will bring people to you or show you where they are stranded."

"Okay, but I'm afraid," I whisper.

"I know you are afraid. You are also humble of heart and know your need for Me. I'll always be with you. I know you have reason to doubt yourself, but have I ever given you a reason to doubt Me?" my Captain gently questions.

And there it is: my moment of truth. Who do I put my faith in? Who holds my trust and whose directions am I going to follow? His or mine? Are fear and doubt going to make my decisions? Or will I follow the One who never leaves me nor forsakes me? Slowly, a peace that surpasses all understanding fills my mind. An inexplicable energy reverberates from my being.

"Yes!" I cry. "Yes!" I laugh. All my time on the boat and my experiences culminate gloriously in this moment.

"With You, my Captain, by my side and with You as my strength, I can do all things!"

With net in hand, I give Him a look of triumph, and then, with confident determination, I march forth down the gangplank.

II
Reveal

I waited and waited and waited for God.
At last he looked; finally he listened.
He lifted me out of the ditch,
pulled me from deep mud.
He stood me up on a solid rock
to make sure I wouldn't slip.
He taught me how to sing the latest God-song,
a praise-song to our God.
More and more people are seeing this:
they enter the mystery,
abandoning themselves to God.

Psalm 40:1-3

We don't understand at the beginning, but as we journey down the river, we gain understanding. We gain knowledge that we are not the captains of our boats. The more we try to be in control, the deeper we find ourselves in the river depths. This river is not ours to direct, no matter how we try to manipulate it, manage it or maneuver in it. In the end, it is God's river.

Within His river, God has a specific purpose and plan for all of our lives. His gold is like a connecting stream of treasure that flows to a fulfillment that only He can create. However, the river flows through this world—and in this world there is darkness and false gold. The world's pyrite lures us away from God's gold nuggets and His stream of treasure. We errantly search after the pyrite, mistaking it for God's gold. Pyrite will never bring us the satisfaction our hearts desire.

God reveals to us a foolproof way to distinguish the world's pyrite from His gold. This unfailing way is through a relationship with Jesus, our Captain. The way of our Captain is the way to eternal living: it is the process of loving Him and loving others. This process is accomplished through the work of the Holy Spirit, God's Navigator, as He guides us through each day. The Navigator is the one who brings Scriptures (verses from the "manual") alive for us so we can gain wisdom and insight into any situation that arises. The Navigator speaks to our hearts, urging us to pray; He tugs and nudges us in our daily living and guides us in our responses to life's challenges.

Where are you in your river journey? How is God revealing Himself to you today?

Are you on the boat with the Captain, not really knowing Him but content to watch Him from afar? Are you satisfied to stay there, not wanting to risk getting too close to Him for fear He will call you to do something you are not comfortable with? Are you doing all the right things but for the wrong reasons?

Are you just stepping out of the boat onto the island? Has the Captain given you a task to accomplish on shore? Are you on the beach, wondering why you need to stay close to the Captain? Are you resting because you have been through a lot and deserve a break? Are you a long way down the path, gathering pyrite and ignoring the guiding signposts? Is your backpack heavy? What's in it?

Are you at the university or church of MM&I (me, myself and I)? Are you following someone or something that has immobilized you? Do you think you have all the answers and are content to sit down? Are you stuck in a tower of comfort? Are you screaming from a turret?

Are you stuck in a circle going around and around, never getting off the well-traveled road because you don't know which path to take? Do you feel like no one is listening to you or helping you? Has a tragedy or a life-altering event forced you onto a path you never wanted to be on? Are you scared and in despair?

Are you at a place where you know you are in danger but, instead of stopping, you keep pushing ahead in the darkness? Or worse, do you feel your feet sinking in the bog with the mud threatening to suck you under? Are you drowning?

No matter where you are in your river journey, you, along with most of us, are searching for treasure to satisfy your desires. This is a constant worldly temptation. Your treasure may look different than ours, but these treasures represent our idea of "making it." Our desires are represented within life's successes. Whether it is money, career, image or relationships, worldly treasure represents the pinnacle of success.

Doesn't success equal satisfaction? Doesn't success equal breaking the tape at the finish line or feeling that you have "arrived"? Whatever success represents for each of us, we all have searched on the Island of Eye or *I* unable to distinguish God's gold from pyrite. These failures on our part *do not* exclude us from the Kingdom. In fact, the more we have stumbled and fallen, the more God's grace works to set us right.

> *Generous in love—God, give grace!*
> *Huge in mercy—wipe out my bad record.*
> *Scrub away my guilt,*
> *soak out my sins in your laundry.*
> *I know how bad I've been;*
> *my sins are staring me down.*
> *You're the One I've violated, and you've seen*
> *it all, seen the full extent of my evil.*
> *You have all the facts before you;*
> *whatever you decide about me is fair.*
> *I've been out of step with you for a long time,*
> *in the wrong since before I was born.*
> *What you're after is truth from the inside out.*
> *Enter me, then; conceive a new, true life.*
>
> Psalm 51:1-6

God's grace is unmerited favor. We don't deserve it, but God gives it to us anyway. His grace is sufficient for each of us. There is nothing too big or awful or wrong that cannot be overcome by it. God's grace is given to us before we even know that it exists.

⌒ ROBIN'S JOURNEY

We were young adults…adventurous, fearless and lacking in wisdom. We all knew of God…not many of us knew God.

It had rained for a week. The swollen creek was muddy and full of unseen and dangerous debris. Why we thought it was a good idea to go canoeing in March is now beyond my comprehension.

As our small group took on the floodwaters, it became apparent that we were on a perilous and dangerous ride. I was very thankful that my future husband was steering our canoe—I had total faith in his abilities. As we maneuvered through a difficult stretch, I heard our friends cry out and turned to see their canoe stuck on debris. My first instinct, which I voiced, was to turn around and assist them. Ted's response was no—if we turn, we will be in trouble, too. He wanted to pull over on the bank and let them try to extract themselves first. I insisted. He relented. I was wrong. He was right.

We turned and immediately got sucked up against a tree that used to be on dry ground. As I leaned, he shouted, "Don't lean!" and with that we were dumped into the raging waters. He yelled, "*Swim!*" as he set out for the bank and safety.

It was cold…so very cold. My mind seemed to slow down. I was not quite thinking clearly. As I floated downstream, my life jacket keeping me afloat, my feet suddenly seemed to hit solid ground. I felt such relief. I was safe. It didn't seem as cold anymore. I situated myself and stood there watching as the others gathered on the bank. I had no concerns since I felt secure on my safe perch in the middle of the rain-swollen, debris-filled, dark and muddy waters.

The sound of the water was deafening. As I looked at the turbulent and angry rapids between the bank and me, I noticed my friends shouting at me. I wondered why, since I was now completely safe. Thinking they did not realize I was actually on stable ground, I did not respond. But they seemed to become more frantic in their calls.

Then I heard him. Ted. This man who loved me. His voice rose above the rest, directing me to swim. I shouted back, "No! It's okay, I'm fine." He locked eyes with me. He was yelling something and motioning to me to cross the rapids. I remember thinking, *Why would I swim across that raging water, when I can just stay here where I am obviously safe?*

He continued to yell. Then he said, *"Robin!"* and started into the raging water. I was shaken. Why was he getting into this dangerous water? Then it dawned on me...he was coming after me...he was risking his life to save mine. But I was safe...why would he do that? I could not let him....

His eyes were still locked with mine. They were speaking volumes. I couldn't look anywhere else. I saw love...I saw concern...I saw determination...I saw strength. Those eyes pleaded with me.

Then, above the roar of the water, I heard his voice, calmly encouraging me, telling me I could do it...I could swim...I could make it; he would help me.

Suddenly, I noticed that I was cold, so very cold. My arms and legs were becoming numb...my mind was registering that something was wrong, terribly wrong. I was not really safe at all. His eyes, his voice, his action suddenly shook me out of my delirium.

It took every bit of strength I had to move myself off my safe perch into those raging waters. It was not because I wanted to, but because I did not want him to get hurt coming after me. In that moment, I made a choice to set fear aside in favor of love. So I pushed out into the raging waters and swam towards Ted, who pulled me to safety.

God's grace was on full display that day. Of course, I did not fully understand that He just saved me from death. But the memory of that event became a navigation point that connected with other points as I continued on my river journey.

Again, where do you think you are in your journey?

Some of us are perched on a perceived safe spot in the midst of a raging river. We are too scared to move off our precarious perch since it is familiar to us, even though it is not the best place for us to be. Others are stuck climbing the tower of success, wanting to get out but unable to find the exit. Many of us are just about to be run over by a stampede of wild horses and need to jump off the path immediately or risk circling through the same disastrous life issues again! Still others are hiding in comfortable boats, not wanting to move outside their very own self-made complacent cocoons where they live in their comforts and pass judgment on the lives of others.

Unfortunately, in all these scenarios we are dangerously close to tragedy. We carry on day after day, searching for this world's pyrite and seeking comfort that never satisfies us. We fail to make the necessary corrections in our lives because we either don't know we need change or we don't know what changes to make. The bottom line is, many of us simply fear change.

The question then becomes, how do we move on from our point in the river?

The answer is, we do so through the love revealed by God in Jesus.

> *Our firm decision is to work from this focused center: One man died for everyone. That puts everyone in the same boat. He included everyone in his death so that everyone could also be included in his life, a resurrection life, a far better life than people ever lived on their own.*
>
> 2 Corinthians 5:14-15

Jesus reveals Himself to us every day. We need to open our eyes so we can recognize the new life He has for us.

III

Recognize

I know you inside and out, and find little to my liking. You're not cold, you're not hot—far better to be either cold or hot! You're stale. You're stagnant. You make me want to vomit. You brag, "I'm rich, I've got it made, I need nothing from anyone," oblivious that in fact you're a pitiful, blind beggar, threadbare and homeless.

Here's what I want you to do: Buy your gold from me, gold that's been through the refiner's fire. Then you'll be rich. Buy your clothes from me, clothes designed in Heaven. You've gone around half-naked long enough. And buy medicine for your eyes from me so you can see, really see.

The people I love, I call to account—prod and correct and guide so that they'll live at their best. Up on your feet, then! About face! Run after God!

Look at me. I stand at the door. I knock. If you hear me call and open the door, I'll come right in and sit down to supper with you. Conquerors will sit alongside me at the head table, just as I, having conquered, took the place of honor at the side of my Father. That's my gift to the conquerors!

Are your ears awake? Listen. Listen to the Wind Words, the Spirit blowing through the churches.

Revelation 3:15-22

Ouch! These are sobering words from the book of Revelation directed to the church of Laodicea. God revealed in this passage specific inequities without any sugarcoating. Frankly, these are scary words, not only for the Church at that time but also for us today. The revealing of our shortcomings is always hard to hear. All of us can benefit from God's intervention in our lives especially if we are journeying in the wrong direction.

We are heading in the wrong direction when we are maneuvering through life oblivious to God's plan. His plan and His gold treasure will be revealed to us through the gentle urging of the Holy Spirit, our Navigator and the Bible, His navigation manual.

Eventually, each of us reaches a point where we question our life choices. Has our life's course been plotted using pyrite? Are we at our breaking point when we no longer trust ourselves to be captain? Recognize this! Jesus is knocking at our door. This point arrives at precise times and is unique to each person. It is a point of truth between God and each of us. Our choice is to turn towards or away from God. The beautiful thing about God is that if we choose to turn away, there will be another point on our journey when a new opportunity to turn towards Him will be presented. God is very persistent in His unconditional love for us.

When we turn towards God, He helps us recognize our need for Jesus as our Captain and the Holy Spirit as our Navigator. He refines us like the He did the church at Laodicea, by bringing to light our flaws, not to punish us but to strengthen us for our journey. He opens our eyes to see our lives through a different perspective, one of His making. By prodding, teaching, correcting and guiding us, He shows us His unconditional love.

When we grasp His extended hand, we begin to realize where we actually are in our journey. This revelation is accomplished through a joint effort of God's prompting and our obedience. God reveals Himself to us while we recognize our need for Him. The way this occurs is unique to each of us. No one's journey is ever the same.

⟨ ROBIN'S JOURNEY

Something was missing. It seemed like every time I thought I had found the missing piece, I returned to the same feeling—the feeling that something was missing.

For many years, I thought the missing piece was a loving relationship. Then I married the love of my life, but the "something" was still missing. I found out before marriage that I had an ongoing medical condition that might prevent me from having children. The minute I found out that I might not be able to have kids, I wanted them desperately. I thought if we had children, I would find what was missing.

We tried to conceive for five years without success. It seemed like getting pregnant was my sole focus. It was a lonely time. It seemed every time I turned around, someone I knew was pregnant. We tried numerous fertility treatments, expended hours of time driving to and from appointments, and spent our extra funds on medical expenses. It was the first time in my life that I could not have what I wanted.

So, when I became pregnant with triplets, I was over the top with joy until we lost one of our children within weeks. The joy turned to sorrow and trepidation. I was terrified, knowing that I had no control over the lives I carried. At four months, we lost our second child. I was distraught and inconsolable. At twenty-eight weeks, I thought my water had broken and was admitted to the hospital. It turned out to be a high leak, so I remained in the hospital on bed rest and began receiving treatments for my baby's lungs. After three weeks of treatments, an ultrasound revealed that the amniotic fluid was dangerously low.

Our beautiful, tiny baby Sarah was born that night, at 3 pounds, 13 ounces. She had no lung issues, and other than a bit of jaundice, appeared to be healthy. As I visited her in the NICU day after day and held her every moment I could, I was overwhelmed by this precious gift.

We brought her home three weeks later with a monitor that would warn us if she stopped breathing at night. Ted and I shared parenting duties and tried to maintain our self-employment as we had done before. Of course, that was impossible. But we had a wonderful safety net of people surrounding us, including family, friends and employees, who all stepped up and shouldered new responsibilities.

I was sure I had finally found the "missing" piece: motherhood. It was life altering. It changed everything, especially my perspective. I wondered if I was actually who I thought I was. But even after a loving marriage and a beautiful child, there it was, that *something else* nagging at me.

Ted and I guffawed when our doctor told us that having one child might kick-start the system. But when we got pregnant again with a due date the same as Sarah's but a year later, I was shocked and incredibly joyful at the same time. I was excited to experience an uneventful full-term pregnancy with no issues and no C-section.

As my due date passed and the contractions increased, my "gut" said to me, "Something is wrong, terribly wrong!" I listened. I called my doctor, and he scheduled me to be induced the next day. I was scared and once again not in control of the world around me.

I arrived at noon, and they hooked me up to the monitor. I could tell from the nurse's expression that it was not good. At 12:05 p.m. she called my doctor. He arrived and told us that our baby was in trouble. She was not breathing properly. As a result, I would have to have an emergency C-section. He said I would be given a general anesthesia, which meant Ted could not stay with me. I was devastated and begged my doctor to let me stay awake with a spinal. He tilted his head and in his British accent quipped, "I will try."

As my British-born obstetrician and my Irish-born anesthesiologist bantered back and forth about what music we should be listening to, I once again realized that I had no control over the life I carried. Our beautiful Rachael entered the world an hour later. Ted was present to greet her as she made her entrance. Later on, I realized *something* had alerted me to seek help. But I didn't dwell on that thought. I lost track of my need for the *something else* as it faded into the overwhelming adventure of parenthood.

Fast-forward four years. Parenting is all consuming! I feel like I forgot large blocks of time during my girls' toddler years. But as they approached ages three and four, I started to sense the *something else is missing* feeling again, and there was a difference. This time I felt an urgency.

My mother suggested that I have the girls baptized. At this point in my river journey, I was a member of a church but never attended except maybe on Christmas Eve and Easter. It's not that I did not believe in God; I just did not even consider Him in my thoughts. He was like a "big" overseer who I did not really need, since I thought I was okay. But this suggestion from my mom nagged at me. I think I actually was offended or maybe just embarrassed that I had never considered it. Regardless, the thought haunted me.

Then my mom told me that there was a new minister at our church and that I might find her interesting. I was surprised because my mom had not attended church in years. I was aware that she did not like many of the pastors who came and went from our church, possibly because she was a PK (preacher's kid) and was always comparing them to my grandfather. Of course, he certainly was someone to aspire to because he was a wonderfully gentle man with great preaching ability. I don't remember any of his sermons in particular, just the peacefully joyful feeling I experienced after listening to him. The feeling of missing *something else* became undeniable and persistent.

I did not know what I was doing or why, but I knew I needed to search. Church seemed like a good place to start. I couldn't remember why I'd left in the first place; maybe I stopped attending because, at the time, it seemed irrelevant and boring. I somehow determined that I had better things to do on Sunday, like pursuing my own pleasures and captaining my own boat. Now it seemed like a good place to start. So, I returned from my twenty-year church hiatus.

Mom was right. The new pastor was good; I hung on to every word she spoke. It seemed like each week her sermon was exactly what I needed to hear. I was excited to go, and so were the girls. I made new friends and got reacquainted with old ones. Since I was taking the girls to Sunday school, I went, too. It was as if a whole new realm opened to me. Stories from my youth took on new meaning as my soul was reawakened.

Several months later, there was an announcement of a small group being formed to experience a journey called "John Wesley's Great Experiment." (See *Ten Brave Christians: The John Wesley Great Experiment—Participant's Primer* by Danny Morris.) It was an experiment in a new way of living. Those thirty days changed the course of my life. I found my *something else*: God!

I turned to Him with my full attention. I actually knew He was listening. Deep in my soul, I knew. I knew that He heard me and I heard

Him. It was the beginning of a lifelong journey of experiencing life with God and His love, moment by moment. I recognized that God meets me in each moment. ~

God continues to help us recognize our need for Him through the movement of the Holy Spirit. The Holy Spirit prompts us internally as well as externally. Internally, the Holy Spirit might nudge us or cause us to pause, similar to how Robin knew something was missing. Externally, the Holy Spirit works through gold gatherers—other people He uses to help us in our journey. Remember, gold gatherers are chosen by Jesus for specific missions to cast their nets to gather God's gold.

TARA'S JOURNEY

Many years ago I was categorized on my medical chart as an AMA (advanced maternal age) first-time mother of a six-month-old son. I chose to work part-time at night at my former full-time day job. I believed this was an optimal solution to my quandary of being a stay-at-home mom who felt she needed to hold a position outside the home that produced an income. I knew my priority was to be a stay-at-home mom, but I had always worked. I didn't know how *not* to have a job. I had picked up the "successful career" pyrite many years before and didn't know how to carry it simultaneously with being a stay-at-home mom. I was determined to do it all!

On a bright Saturday morning, I was taking myself to the moms' group at church to hear an RN who was the featured speaker. The schedule stated that she would be sharing home remedies for common illnesses for children. For example, teething can cause diarrhea. Some doctors won't tell you this, but it is true.

I can remember the decision to attend this gathering was extremely stressful for me. Should I attend or not attend? It was a moms' group, for heaven's sake, not rocket science, but decisions of this nature were agonizing for me. Why? Because I was faced with choosing to leave my child in order to socialize, and that seemed frivolous to me. On the other hand, leaving him to go to work and produce income seemed valuable. There I was again, picking up more pyrite. So, in my mind socializing was unacceptable while producing income was acceptable. I remember convincing myself that this gathering was not socializing; this was a recon mission for medical knowledge to help my child.

That probably sounds like a very crazy way of thinking, but I was very crazy at that time. Here's why. My baby and I never slept. Well, he slept, but not for more than two hours at a time *while I was at home.* His longest sleeping time was in the evenings from 6:00 p.m. to 11:30 p.m., which were the very same hours that I was at work. Common symptoms of sleep deprivation are mood changes, difficulty concentrating, impaired performance, memory problems, disorientation, hallucinations and paranoia. That's just the cocktail every first-time mom should drink on a daily basis, right?

A large component to our son's sleeping habits was that he was born five weeks early. He needed to spend a week in the hospital for issues related to jaundice. Because of his early entry into the world, we came home to an incomplete second-floor nursery. We had to make a new nursery in the living room along with his "biliblanket."

A biliblanket or bilirubin blanket is a home phototherapy system that treats some degrees of jaundice. The blanket has fiber optics in the fabric that generate light that helps break down the bilirubin in the baby's body. When a baby is on or wrapped in a biliblanket, the little one takes on the appearance of a glowworm toy. It is very cute but not effective for swaddling. The fiber optics in the blanket don't allow for the snugness consistent with the swaddling method, and our son needed to be on the biliblanket as much as physically possible.

So, swaddling wasn't an option. Neither was our son sleeping on his stomach. Why? Well, he couldn't be laid on his stomach because I was sure my *first-time mom crazy ears* heard the hospital staff say that if you allowed an infant to lie on his stomach, he would die. Yes, my mind instantly heard *die*, so that left me with only one option. My sweet baby slept on my chest with the biliblanket on top of him. Please allow yourself to laugh out loud at my expense!

Let's get back to my story of the moms' group event. I was a first-time, sleep-deprived mom prepped to superficially socialize, with notebook at the ready. Enter Terri. Terri was a longtime member of our church and had been a practicing RN for more than twenty-five years. She had four grown children of her own and was almost a grandmother. Terri was a soft-spoken, witty woman with dancing blue eyes. Her laugh sounded like a bubbling brook, and she exuded an air of grace and respect. I was instantly entranced, at least for a few moments.

Terri started her talk by explaining that the Lord had shifted her topic for the day. Her topic had changed from home remedies to unconditional love. *This was not on my agenda.* She spoke on how we are to love our children unconditionally as our Heavenly Father loves us. *What? How could a checklist be created out of that?*

As time seemed to stand still, she laughed as she told stories of her children. She stated that if she could go back in time, she would go back to the period when her four children were all under the age of twelve. She smiled as she said that no matter what the weather, she would dress everyone up two times daily and go outside. *How is that even possible? I can barely care for an infant who doesn't even move yet, and she is glowing about prepping four children to go outside in any weather! Any weather!* She giggled about rainy days and snowy weather. *Rain? Really? Rain produces mud and can turn into snow. Well, snow is cold, and there's probably wind! She must be a superhero.* I was mesmerized.

Terri spoke of herself as a morning person. She loved to get up early in the morning and have quiet time. She cherished this extra time in the morning for devotions and the peaceful start to her day. However, when her children were small, her early morning time was forfeited to fatigue because she would stay up too late cleaning and picking things up. She would spend hours making sure all projects were done and her home was set and in order. Her personal peace was the casualty of the fresh-page approach with her home. She explained that by staying up much later than the children at night to "right" things, she sacrificed her own energy and positive outlook for the morning. If she had the chance to do it again, she said, "I would just put myself to sleep."

Sleep? If she could do it again, she would put herself to *sleep! I don't sleep. I try to sleep when my baby sleeps, but it is not enough! When he does sleep, I'm at work. I'm so exhausted.* The thought of sleep was glorious!

I practically ran home from the meeting and announced to my husband, Mike, that I needed to quit my job to get more sleep. His loving response was to kiss my forehead and say, "I wondered when you were going to figure that out." He had previously weighed the hit we would take to our finances if I wasn't working and knew we could get by. I am grateful for his wisdom and patience as I journeyed through this decision and came to the conclusion in my own time. I threw the pyrite labeled "your value is measured by making money" out the window in that moment.

God used that moms' group event to put me in a place to learn to listen—not to hear what my adult ears planned to listen to, but to hear and recognize what He had for me. In the past, I would have stopped listening because she was not saying what I had come to hear. God led me to listen like a child, setting my adult agenda aside. I listened and appreciated the gold gatherer He sent to me. Terri cooperated with God and shifted her topic in order to work in God's will and His way. I'm so thankful that she listened. Her talk was, for me, from God.

Time moved on, life happened, and the Holy Spirit continued to move.

My oldest son was now almost four years old. We had added a daughter to the mix, who was now almost two years old, and I was pregnant for the third time, due in December. My mother called and asked if my sister and I would consider accompanying her to the Women of Faith Conference later that year. It was a two-day, one-night bus trip, and I would be home by Saturday evening.

Whoa! Stop the press! Was she suggesting I could go away, overnight? Recheck the stats in the earlier paragraph. I had a four-year-old, a two-year-old and a baby on the way. Although I had overcome my earlier sleeping issue and had gained a good chunk of control over my first-time mom crazies, my order and my plans were still paramount. I couldn't conceive of creating, let alone explaining to Mike, the checklist that would need to be followed if I were gone for two days. Inconceivable! I regretfully declined the invitation from Mother by stating there was no possible way for me to be away from my family for that amount of time.

Fast-forward to early the next year. Mother called again to ask if my sister and I would accompany her to the Women of Faith Conference later in September. Whoa! Stop the press! Recheck the stats, Mom. I now have an almost five-year-old, an almost three-year-old, and a two-month-old. You want me to set aside my parenting duties and desert my family overnight?!

That sounded absolutely glorious!

I remember thinking, *I'm sure this Women of Faith meeting/convention thing will be fine, but, oh my, getting to spend almost two days and a night away from home sounds like a Calgon commercial!* I couldn't remember the last time I had an uninterrupted conversation, let alone actual adult time. Right there was my motivation—adult-only time away, plus the best company in the world! Even if the speakers were uninspiring, I was happy to just sit through their presentation and pass the time.

My boat in the river was about to dock as the Lord led me to the Women of Faith Conference to teach me how to see. At the conference, I had my first experience with seeing a large group gathered solely to worship our Lord. Enter Sheila Walsh, Patsy Clairmont, Marilyn Meberg, Lisa Harper and Dr. Henry Cloud. This is not an all-inclusive list of the talent at my first Women of Faith Conference, but they were the heavy hitters in my memory bank. These ladies and gentleman were sharing testimonies as well as wisdom, laughter, tears and song. They were sharing the message of God and His love for us in a way that my eyes had never seen before. It was powerful and ignited my soul! My eyes were opened to see real women using speaking and musical gifts to captivate and energize an audience and, above all, praise the Lord. They were fearless!

Many puzzle pieces of my past collided within me when I looked down at the ladies on the stage and around at the people in the arena. In my life experience before motherhood, I was a professional speaker and trainer for a large corporation—but it had nothing to do with Jesus. So, what was He trying to get me to recognize? How do I apply my passion for Jesus through these gifts in everyday life? I began to recognize the path He was creating for me: speakers, worship, passion, oh my! I could never have prepared myself for the flooding of possibilities the Lord allowed me to see at my first Women of Faith Conference.

The external movement of the Holy Spirit through people placed in my path created a new awareness for me that opened up a whole new realm of possibilities. I was listening for Him, and I was seeing Him move in the circumstances of each day. I recognized my need to be in constant communication with Him.

As we begin to accept that God is always revealing Himself to us in this day, we recognize our need for Him in the moment-by-moment journey that we are on. This recognition is brought about by the Holy Spirit internally speaking to our hearts and minds. These are moments when we sense God and our need for Him. If we listen, we can hear God's gentle wooing. As He woos us, God works externally through circumstances, using His gold gatherers to get our attention. This process of drawing us to Him is unique for each of us. No one has the same wooing process.

As we recognize our need for Him, He also brings about an awareness of the areas of life where we are not following Him. If we make our choice for God, then our failure to follow Him produces conflicts within us. Sometimes we easily resolve the conflicts by following God. At other times we can't seem to make it through the conflict on our own. We take two steps forward only to fall back into pyrite-seeking behaviors that we thought we had long since overcome.

> *Open up before GOD, keep nothing back; he'll do whatever needs to be done.*
>
> Psalm 37:5

IV

Rebel

*But I need something **more**! For if I know the law but still can't keep it, and if the power of sin within me keeps sabotaging my best intentions, I obviously need help! I realize that I don't have what it takes. I can will it, but I can't **do** it. I decide to do good, but I don't **really** do it; I decide not to do bad, but then I do it anyway. My decisions, such as they are, don't result in actions. Something has gone wrong deep within me and gets the better of me every time.*

It happens so regularly that it's predictable. The moment I decide to do good, sin is there to trip me up. I truly delight in God's commands, but it's pretty obvious that not all of me joins in that delight. Parts of me covertly rebel, and just when I least expect it, they take charge.

I've tried everything and nothing helps. I'm at the end of my rope. Is there no one who can do anything for me? Isn't that the real question?

The answer, thank God, is that Jesus Christ can and does. He acted to set things right in this life of contradictions where I want to serve God with all my heart and mind, but am pulled by the influence of sin to do something totally different.

Romans 7:17-25

The problem is, we can't control sin on our own. Remember what enticed our traveler in the parable to proceed further down the path on the Isle of I before she drowned? Her only instruction from the Captain was to "stay close," but she didn't. She knew what was right but rebelled. Each step away from the boat was an act of rebellion. On our own river journeys, we justify our actions or choices based on our desires for pyrite or worldly pleasures. In that process, we find ourselves continually being pulled back into sin.

Sin is separation from God. The consequence of sin is death (see Romans 6:23).

In the beginning, sin was introduced when Adam and Eve disobeyed God's command. Their choice separated all people from God. This separation continued through history when God gave the "law" that is spelled out in the Ten Commandments and defined and explained by Moses and the prophets. The law consisted of rules for daily living. If people followed the rules, they would be in step with God. However, the law was circumvented and perverted so that even in its perfection, people who claimed to follow it fell into sin. Once again, people failed and thus remained separated from God.

So, what did God do? He sent His only Son, Jesus, to take sin upon Himself to bridge the separation and reconnect us to God forever. That reconnection by God is called grace. It is nothing we deserve or fully understand.

This is how much God loved the world: He gave his Son, his one and only Son. And this is why: so that no one need be destroyed; by believing in him, anyone can have a whole and lasting life. God didn't go to all the trouble of sending his Son merely to point an accusing finger, telling the world how bad it was. He came to help, to put the world right again. Anyone who trusts in him is acquitted; anyone who refuses to trust him has long since been under the death sentence without knowing it. And why? Because of that person's failure to believe in the one-of-a-kind Son of God when introduced to him.

John 3:16-18

We want to give our rebellion to God; we want Him to take it from us. We want to reconnect with Him, but we don't fully understand the process. Our journey down the river is not a tale of His efforts to make us better. Rather, it is our personal life story of our joint effort with God to rid us of what separates us from Him. It is in this joint navigational process that we understand our need for our Captain. It is in the storms that we truly learn how to rely on Jesus. It is in that reliance that we overcome our rebellion, and it is in the deep waters of doubt that we gain faith.

If this is a joint effort, then how did we lose God in our river journey? How did we get so far off course? We rebel by going off on our own. The world is constantly promoting self-love, which is basically putting our personal wants and desires above everything else. For example, worldly self-love tells us that our happiness is paramount over anyone else's feelings. "I deserve it" is a common excuse to do whatever feels good. Our own knowledge and logic trump all else. Self-love is the misguided belief that we know what is best for us all the time.

Once we knowingly or unknowingly disregard and relinquish God in favor of this world's distractions, we assume the mutinous captain's role. We are never the true captain of our boat. The Captain is still with us, but we have disregarded Him as irrelevant when charting our course. We are using the wrong navigation manual, the wrong guide and the wrong tools.

We are trying to define ourselves through the world's filter instead of through God's plan. This incorrect process results in the establishment of life patterns using our "self" compass. We err when it comes to setting goals and making life choices, because God's wisdom does not even factor into our pros and cons list. It is all about us. The course we set to achieve life goals using the self-love approach results in the accumulation of pyrite.

For example, attaining wealth is a life goal for most of us. Money is needed to purchase basic necessities like shelter, food and clothing. In abundance, it also buys luxuries such as the latest gadgets, vacations and education. It appears that the more money we have, the more self-satisfied we should be. Are we?

Another life goal is securing relationships. Humans are created to be in loving, accepting relationships. However, the world defines the "gold" standard of relationships as a Barbie and Ken marriage with 2.4 kids, or being raised by Ward and June Cleaver or Will and Kate. It appears that if you have one of the world's "gold-standard" relationships, you will be self-satisfied. Is this always true?

Many of us focus on pursuing our passion as a life goal. Embedded within us are special gifts and talents that make each of us unique individuals. The world's "gold standard" for our gifts and talents involve comparisons with others to rank whose talent is number one in the field, who is the best and the brightest, or who is the top dog. It appears that if we reach the top of our field or are considered the best at what we do, we will be self-satisfied. Are we?

Most of us pursue these self-satisfying life goals according to the world's compass as opposed to achieving God's goals for us through His compass.

So, look at this equation: if gold equals life goals, reaching life goals equals success, and achieving success brings about satisfaction, then gold equals satisfaction. Right? Wrong! This type of satisfaction is fleeting because the treasure is merely pyrite.

Let's go back to the Isle of I. Our traveler never made a decision with the thought that it was a bad decision. Remember when she was picking up treasure and putting the gold in her backpack? She picked up so much that she unloaded her navigation essentials to get more treasure. In reality, wrong decision-making is the process of picking up pyrite. Pyrite is a decision made without God. The satisfaction we get from it is temporary at best. With regard to the accumulation of money, relationships, careers or anything else, eventually decisions made without God fail to satisfy.

On our own river journeys, we decide what is gold according to our own self-interest. No one takes risks to pick up pyrite. We justify those risks in order to attain what we want without consulting God. Why would we do that? Self-love camouflages the heart of a rebel who maintains control.

Let's be clear. Many of us believe that we do consult God on a much larger, distant scale. For example, we talked about money, relationships and careers. On that distant scale, these categories do involve God. God knows we need money for basic necessities. He built us for relationships, and He has given each of us talents that we can channel into a livelihood. Our rebellion comes in our failure to consult and follow God's direction in the daily process of life. Going to church on Sunday does not mean that we consult God on Monday.

Walking through the details of everyday life is similar to a connect-the-dot picture. The dots make up our navigation map or course. It makes a difference who is in charge of the navigation process as we connect the dots to move to the next location on the map. Is it Jesus or us? When "self" becomes the captain of the navigation process, then we openly disregard or lose sight of the true Captain. Doing so produces a map that is filled with incorrectly connected or disconnected dots, resulting in an unrecognizable picture. We end up feeling lost and carrying a heavy backpack of pyrite.

God brought us to this point. Do we hear Him? Are we recognizing the internal nudging of the Holy Spirit? Is the Navigator showing us externally through circumstances and people which direction to go? In our rebellious control, are we ignoring these guiding signposts? When we begin to feel God's urgings within our soul, they produce conflict and confusion with our self-love approach to life. Even though the self-love approach leaves us dissatisfied and wanting, we tend to have trouble breaking free of this default behavior, especially when we are under stress.

JONAH'S JOURNEY

Most people remember only the swallowing of Jonah by the big fish. But if you haven't read the book of Jonah recently, reading it again will give you the ability to put yourselves in Jonah's shoes.

Jonah, an Old Testament prophet, was in great conflict and distress because he was confused about who should be navigating: himself or God.

Basically, God speaks audibly to Jonah and says, "Go to Nineveh."

Jonah says, "No, I don't want to go to Nineveh because they are a mean, awful people. I don't want to be associated with them. I am uncomfortable with their lifestyle and how they treat You, God. They need to be destroyed, but I'm sure You will find a way to forgive them!"

Jonah chooses his own self-righteousness over God's decree and takes off in the opposite direction from Nineveh. He is shipwrecked because of his disobedience and swallowed by the big fish. Now, he is in a pickle. Whose hand does he reach for? God's hand, of course.

God says, "I told you to go to Nineveh."

Jonah says, "God, I am so sorry. If You forgive me, I will go to Nineveh now."

The big fish spits him out after three days, and Jonah goes to Nineveh. When he gets there, Jonah gives God's message to the Ninevites, and, lo and behold, they repent! As Jonah predicted, God, in His mercy, forgives them.

Jonah's response is *anger*! He is now angry that God is showing them mercy. He is of the opinion that they do not deserve God's mercy. He seems to forget the mercy that God just showed him by removing him from the belly of the big fish. Jonah moves to a hillside above the city to stew in his self-righteous indignation. He still thinks God might listen to his opinion and destroy the Ninevites.

God continues to pursue Jonah. He plants a tree to shade Jonah on the hillside so he can be comfortable. Jonah is more than willing to accept this merciful act of God and the comfort it brings. He enjoys the shade of the tree and gives glory to God for it. Yet, he doesn't understand that God is showing him mercy (yet again).

As Jonah sits and waits for the destruction of Nineveh that he hopes is coming, the shade tree given to him withers and dies. All Jonah can think about is "woe is me."

> GOD said, "What's this? How is it that you can change your feelings from pleasure to anger overnight about a mere shade tree that you did nothing to get? You neither planted nor watered it. It grew up one night and died the next night. So, why can't I likewise change what I feel about Nineveh from anger to pleasure, this big city of more than 120,000 childlike people who don't yet know right from wrong, to say nothing of all the innocent animals?"
>
> Jonah 4:10-11

God concludes Jonah's story by humbling him into recognizing his own self-absorption. Jonah was more distraught about the loss of his shade than the destruction of 120,000 people.

Do we see ourselves in Jonah's judgment of others? Do we see ourselves in Jonah's disregard of God's plan in favor of his opinion of the Ninevites? Do we see our rebellion as easily as it is to see his?

TARA'S JOURNEY

Unlike Jonah, God did not tell me to go to Nineveh. God did not tell me anything, for I was not consulting God. I was in my early twenties (many years prior to Mike and motherhood) and not listening for God's voice or guidance. Please keep in mind, I knew I was in the river and loved by God, and I loved Him. I knew God's rules and was more than happy to follow them *as long as* they aligned with what I wanted and felt was right for me.

Similar to Jonah, I was exclusively in control of all of my life's decision-making. When a life choice presented itself, I made my list of pros and cons. When God's direction ended up as a con, I didn't consider God wrong; I just felt that I knew more than God did. No one knows what's best for me better than me, right? Unfortunately, it took more than one big fish to set me straight.

I hold a firm belief that there is not a person on this earth who ever gets married with the intent of getting divorced. Divorce is the necessary evil of this world to stop abuse, to break a commitment, or to nullify a contract that God never signed. Marriage is of God; it is His creation and design between a man and a woman and Himself, as it is written. Having a committed relationship and being married was something I coveted. When you get married, that means someone must love you above all else, right?

Have you heard the saying, "God was invited to the wedding but not into the marriage"? I believe this saying applied to me tenfold. For even if you attend church, take part in marriage counseling, and have a wedding in a church, nowhere does that guarantee that you have invited God into the marriage. All of those items can be put on a checklist of the "right things" to do when *you* decide to get married. When all the right things have been marked off on your checklist, down the aisle you go.

The "married" pyrite lost its shine faster than I could remove my false eyelashes. Immaturity in many aspects of life can bring out this dulling effect for many young couples. Our greatest immaturity was our faith in God. God had zero influence on any of the decisions we were making in our lives; consequently, we did not have any fortitude to maintain let alone survive the relationship. We talked the talk, but we weren't walking the walk.

We were divorced in a little over two years, and I was shattered. Divorce left a hollow vastness inside of me. I reached a destination of shame and failure. The details during the transport don't really matter. My feelings of doubt and mistrust towards others were heightened as well as my natural survival instincts. Every movement was work, every day was a chore, and only time began to heal those raw emotions.

The chaos of the thundering wild horses descended into the circle, and I jumped out of the way, falling with great force to the ground. The air was knocked out of me. It was so hard to breathe, and for the first week after my divorce, I prayed for the Lord to take me in my sleep. That was not in His plan. I slowly gained a little strength through the encouragement of a trusted girlfriend, the love of my parents, and the loyalty of my beloved hound.

Life moved on. I felt older and smarter, and I was determined to not make a bad choice again. So, like Jonah when he came out of the big fish, I claimed my errors, took responsibility and vowed to not make the same mistakes twice. My momentum down my new path was growing in leaps and bounds, and that's when it struck me! The easiest way for me to erase this awful stain of "divorced" was to get back to "married" again. With renewed vigor, I held on to my resolve for a gold-filled life and went searching for a gold-standard relationship like never before.

On a new and beautiful path, a giant gold prize in sight, I ran right into a new marriage that was 180 degrees opposite from my first. In this marriage, I didn't bother "talking any talk"! I had no lofty goals to attain, no societal measurement and therefore no need to "walk any walk." Once again, I married in a church, believing God was looking down with approval on how I was managing my life.

Looking back, I can see I never invited God into my decision-making process. Instead, I relied on comparisons to past experiences to bring me comfort. Everything in this marriage that involved expectations and goals was opposite to my first marriage. I wasn't making the same decisions, but that didn't mean I was making the right decisions. I'm sure the devil laughed and laughed and even got a side stitch from watching the tenacity with which I pursued relationship pyrite. To make matters worse, I added the abuse of alcohol to my second marriage.

"Where are you?" He whispered in my ear.

"What? Who?" I didn't recognize the voice at first. "Oh, it's You, God. I'm right here, trying to figure out how to sneak my whiskey-based, Kool-Aid concoction into work at 7:00 a.m. I think this cup is big enough; no one will smell a thing."

"Where are you?" He whispered. "I am waiting for you."

"*What am I doing,* trying to sneak alcohol into work at 7:00 a.m.? Tara, where are you?" I asked myself.

"I am with you," He whispered.

In less than two and a half years, I had met, married and divorced. Again. That's two divorces within six years. After my Lord saved and carried me from the bog the first time, I turned and ran right back into the chaos of the thundering wild horses. There is no fixing this stain. It is forever. Unbelievably, He stood patiently with outstretched arms, waiting for me. I turned to Him again with anxious fright and harried confusion and begged Him to get me out of the mess I'd made of my life again.

He stood strong and weathered the bombardment of the emotions I hurled at Him. Desperation, shame and guilt were my closest companions. To complicate matters, I had just raised myself to a unique level in our community. Most of my high school acquaintances were just getting married for the first time, and here I was getting divorced for the second. I may as well have been a leper. I would have been the first to call out to people to stay away. "Unclean! Unclean!"

I had one critical life decision left. Who was going to be in control? It was time to face my rebellion. Was it going to be me or was it going to be God? My decision-making track record was glaringly awful, so with no other recourse and no trust left in myself, I turned my life decisions over to God. I'd love to be able to say that I did it gratefully with much thanksgiving and praise, but I cannot. Just as Jonah was angry that God was not going to smite the Ninevites, I was angry that God was going to be in charge.

I railed at Him, "Take it! Take it! You go ahead and make all the decisions, and when the next decision goes wrong, *it is Your fault.* I'm putting You first, I'll ask for Your guidance going forward, and I will not look for, let alone pick up, any gold again!" I continued my tirade. "This won't work, though; I'm sure You will mess it up just like me. Then I can officially quit. You are my last option, and when You fail, I will be permitted to check out of this horrid, wretched life with no guilt. Go ahead, do Your worst."

Accepting "God's worst" for my life was the best decision I ever made. It's been over twenty years since my life was full of shame and misery and feeling alone. I traded that self-reliant, insecure life for a life of freedom and security—a life led by my Captain. Since I began allowing God to be in control of my decisions and since I started following Him, He has blessed me with the life He had always planned for me. ～

Tara's journey is full of obvious rebellion that filled her backpack with pyrite. She wanted to be in control, so she consulted God only as a last resort when she got stuck in the bog with the mud and muck rising above her head. Her independent life journey removed God from the navigational process. When she recognized her need for God to be in control of this process, she began to cooperate on a joint journey with God.

However, even when we are on our joint journey with God, we can be sidelined by subtle rebellion. It can creep into our situations and divert us when we least expect it. Remember, we are all on individual journeys. The important thing is to ask God in this day to identify where our rebellion lies. When we know it is rearing its ugly head, we can turn from it through cooperation with God. In that co-operation, God converts rebellion to a signpost of prevention.

ELIJAH'S JOURNEY

It is helpful if you read Elijah's story in chapters 18 and 19 of First Kings and put yourself in his shoes.

Elijah also heard from God in a very big way, but he struggled with rebellion of a different sort. He forgot to trust, resulting in a subtle form of rebellion.

Elijah is a mighty prophet who hears from God audibly. Knowing there would be a drought, Elijah prophesies this message to the Israelites and King Ahab. King Ahab is married to the evil Queen Jezebel, who worships Baal (Satan). After sharing the prophecy, Elijah goes into hiding.

After three years of drought, Ahab is desperate to find provisions for his people and cattle. God calls, and Elijah returns to the scene, offering up a contest. In one corner are the prophets of Baal, and in the other corner is God. Elijah explains, "We are going to build an altar and offer a sacrifice and see whether Baal or God starts the fire. I will even let the Baal prophets go first."

The 450 Baal prophets go to work trying to get Baal to light the fire. Elijah makes fun of them, taunting them as they spend all day trying to get the fire started. All the Israelites are watching.

Then it is Elijah's turn. He rebuilds the altar and tells the Israelites to pour water over the altar three times until it is drenched and the trench surrounding the altar is full. Elijah prays to God, and God lights up the altar, the sacrifice and even the water in the trenches. The Israelites fall in worship to the only true God, God Almighty. Elijah is completely confident and fully trusting in God's abilities to overcome the nonsense worship of Baal.

After this great victory, Elijah prays, God sends the rain, and the drought ends. Meanwhile, Ahab returns to Jezebel, explains the defeat of Baal, and tells what God has done. Jezebel, enraged, sends a death message to Elijah.

How did Elijah respond to Jezebel's message just after God's awesome victory and display of power? He does the unthinkable: he runs away scared. What happened to the confidence that he just displayed? We can only surmise that he succumbed to his human frailness. In his exhaustion and euphoria at watching God at work, Elijah somehow lost his trust in God. He ran straight into a different form of rebellion. He forgot to trust.

✎ ROBIN'S JOURNEY

It was a difficult time. The fire had destroyed the attic, which had fallen onto the second floor before the fire was stopped. The first floor looked like it would be all right—that is, until we returned the next day and saw the water damage. Fortunately, not all was lost. The firefighters had done an incredible job saving what they could and sorting through debris until they found each of the kids' blankets and favorite stuffed animals.

The thing I remember so many years later is the thankfulness I felt that my husband, Ted, and my children were safe. Nothing else seemed to matter as I drove home after "the call." All I wanted to do was see their faces and hug them close to me. When I arrived, I saw what seemed like hundreds of firefighters and neighbors hauling our belongings out of the first floor while the fire raged overhead. I saw my neighbor Ed, his sons and their extended families loading their hay wagon with furniture, pictures, paintings and the dining room chandelier. A firefighter from the town I grew up in more than twenty minutes away took me by the shoulders and asked me what room our computer was in so he could save it, which he did.

After picking up my sons at home and viewing the devastation, I drove to the school to pick up our daughters, who were in second and third grades. On the way, I could only feel thankful that they were safe at school and that Ted and our friend George had saved my preschool sons from the fire. I remember saying to the girls that we may have lost our house, but we would never lose our home. Home is where your family is, and ours was together. It was an all-consuming lesson in "things don't really matter."

Then the next day came. It was a struggle to remember that "things don't really matter" because they had to be dealt with. They had to be inventoried, reported to the insurance company, sorted into the throw-away pile or the salvage pile, and either disposed of, cleaned or moved to some other location.

Questions bombarded us. Our family and friends asked how they could help. What clothing sizes did we need? Should we launder and dry clean the clothing or buy them new? Did we turn off the electricity, the telephone, the internet? Where should they deliver the mail? What was the process to file the claim for insurance for the personal property? Should we rebuild or walk away? In the meantime, should we secure the structure that was still standing? Should the kids go to school the next day?

Fortunately, my parents, who lived twenty-five minutes away, had room to take us all in. We had a safety net of family that surrounded us in an instant. I later learned that Ted's mother had taken all the pictures that were found and laid them out to dry, preserving many of our wedding pictures and childhood photos.

I was overwhelmed. I needed help. Nothing I could do could take this away, and nothing I could do would fix the situation in the short term. I had no control over anything except my response. And yet, I knew deep in my soul that everything would be okay. I did not know how, but there was a certainty that permeated my soul. I could only take one day at a time. Peace could only be found moment by moment.

The day of the fire turned into the next day after the fire. Then the next day after the fire turned into the week after the fire. I watched in awe as my community surrounded us. Each one did what seemed to them a small thing, but to us it meant everything. Betsy, my dear childhood friend, babysat the boys for days on end while Ted and I tried to figure things out. The girls had a ride to school with our friend, Janet, who worked there. My friends picked up bags of clothing that were salvaged and managed to wash them. Other friends donated every conceivable piece of clothing we needed in the short term. Still others helped us pick through the debris and salvage what we could. We were able to laugh and joke that God had a sense of humor, since He allowed this to happen on Ash Wednesday!

Then Ron, our neighbor and a Good Samaritan, stopped by. He asked a simple question: Do you need any help cleaning up? He said he could have a team there on Saturday. Ted and I looked at each other and said yes. Ron arrived on Saturday with forty people from his church and our community. Our church family arrived with food to feed all the workers. In six hours, all the dry wall, insulation and debris had been removed and the house was broom clean.

We were able to stand on the second floor and look up at the clear February sky and give thanks. God had given us hope through His family, the hope we needed to rebuild. I was confident in the provision of God and His love for me.

The rebuilding process began. What seemed like never-ending questions turned into what seemed like never-ending decision-making. After weeks of searching and being offered a lovely, newly renovated cabin nearby that just seemed too good for a family with four small children, we were able to get emergency housing from a disaster-relief company. What a sight to see a three-bedroom mobile home being pulled across my neighbor's field and parked by our chicken coop.

I don't remember shedding a tear until they dug up the only thing that was left untouched on the property: a small portion of grass behind our house. But there was no other way to connect the water and electric unless they dug a trench. The wear and tear of the last six weeks was beginning to take its toll. I started to feel sorry for myself. Rebellion called my name.

I wrote the following in my journal on April 3, 2002:

> *I sat with God in tears today after reading Henri Nouwen's passage from* Gracias! A Latin American Journal *on his hour spent each day at the Carmelite Chapel. He said God must be pleased that he shows up every day to share all his hopes, fears and distractions with Him—the hour is full of distractions and inner restlessness, sleepiness, confusion and boredom. It seldom pleases his senses. But somehow, somewhere he senses God's presence because of his remarkable desire to return. He feels God touches him during that hour in ways he can't see or feel but manifest themselves weeks later. "I realize that something is happening that is so deep that it becomes like the riverbed though which the waters can safely flow and find their way to the open sea."[1] I needed to hear that today as I struggle with every*

aspect of my life from parenthood to my relationship with Ted, from work challenges to all the demands of the house project.

Rebellion was stopped when I turned to God.

But then I quickly turned back. I heard my name called again—calling me to return to myself; calling me to rebel; distracting me from where my focus should be.

My journal entry from April 24, 2002, reads:

Dear God: I have wondered where you are at times. I have experienced some anger at my circumstances—living in this trailer on top of one another, rain pounding down, my husband at work, my friends and family asking what they can do but no one doing anything. I can't think to ask for help but I need it. Only you have heard my cries and so the anger has subsided and the sorrow has returned and the desperate search for strength to help stem the tide of my impatience with the kids, with Ted, with me. This burden seems overwhelming when I look ahead to the next six months. So I try to focus on each day. But by the end of the day, I realize a day is too big to focus on. I need to maybe deal with an hour at a time, trying to relish each moment—to make each moment holy. You have told me this is possible, but I don't know that I'm the right person for the job. Aren't my worries too extensive for a holy moment?

Now that I think about it, my mind only has the capacity for so many worries. I seemed to have substituted the bigger worries of today with the smaller worries of yesterday.

[As I was writing these hypothetical questions into my journal, the Holy Spirit spoke to my soul, giving me insight. I want to emphasize that the following conversation was how I responded to what I perceived the Spirit was speaking to me, not in verbal words, but in discernment given to me.]

…

It doesn't seem that all worries are the same.

…

It's my response that makes the difference! Really?! Then, I need strength to respond to these bigger worries.

…

55

WHAT! You have already given me the strength? When?

…

You're right, of course. I shouldn't be thinking "woe is me," but don't I have the "right" to feel this way, given the circumstances?

…

WHAT! You ask me what my circumstances are? You want me to list them?

…

Okay. Here it goes.
My house burned down.

…

Yes, but I'm now living in a 3 bedroom trailer going crazy because of the closeness.

…

Yes, but I don't want a trailer. It's very nice, and it has furniture, heat, AC, refrigerator, new washer/dryer, 2 full bathrooms, microwave, TV/VCR, and we have clothing.

…

Yes, we are overseeing the rebuilding effort and working with excellent contractors.

…

Yes, our neighbors are very supportive.

…

I'm feeling like this is a fruitless exercise, God. You win.

…

You ARE right, of course. This is not about winning or losing. I'm already winning because I've come to you and you will care for me NOW and ALWAYS. I guess I AM doing all right, Lord. Thank you for all you have given me yesterday, today and tomorrow. I do love you.

Mercy shown. Rebellion quashed. Trust renewed. ～⌣

Rebellion can happen to us when we have wandered off on our own adventures as well as when we are in the boat with Jesus. It stems from our desire to keep control of our lives to ourselves. Rebellion is trusting in our own abilities instead of trusting in God's strength. It is failing to trust that He will never leave us or forsake us. It is failing to trust that His plans are to prosper us and not to harm us, to give us hope and a future (see Jeremiah 29:11).

Rebellion can be obvious; it also can be subtle. It plagues us throughout our journey and distracts us from following the Captain. It is not enough to believe in God. We must believe God.

> *Keep your eyes on **Jesus**, who both began and finished this race we're in. Study how he did it. Because he never lost sight of where he was headed—that exhilarating finish in and with God—he could put up with anything along the way: Cross, shame, whatever. And now he's **there**, in the place of honor, right alongside God. When you find yourselves flagging in your faith, go over that story again, item by item, that long litany of hostility he plowed through. **That** will shoot adrenaline into your souls!*
>
> *In this all-out match against sin, others have suffered far worse than you, to say nothing of what Jesus went through—all that bloodshed! So don't feel sorry for yourselves. Or have you forgotten how good parents treat children, and that God regards you as **his** children?*
>
> Hebrews 1:2-5

Identification of our own rebellion, telling God about it, and asking for forgiveness and guidance enables us to overcome it. When identification occurs, we can start to turn from it, and that opens up a choice for us. Are we ready to give up ourselves and what we want for what God wants for us? When our answer is "yes!" our hearts recognize our total need for God. We recognize the ugliness in ourselves and the need to be rid of it. We feel deep sorrow and want God to cleanse us and make us new.

That is repentance—when we turn from our rebellion, recognize the error of our ways, and ask God to forgive and cleanse us. This process releases us from self-condemnation and rids us of the garbage that threatens to accumulate. God is able to redeem us and turn what we once were into something new. When we truly want His way in our hearts, minds and souls, then we can forge ahead on the path He has set for us as His new creation.

> *As long as you did what you felt like doing, ignoring God,*
> *you didn't have to bother with right thinking or right living,*
> *or right **anything** for that matter. But do you call that a free*
> *life? What did you get out of it? Nothing you're proud of now.*
> *Where did it get you? A dead end.*
>
> *But now that you've found you don't have to listen to sin tell you*
> *what to do, and have discovered the delight of listening to God*
> *telling you, what a surprise! A whole, healed, put-together life*
> *right now, with more and more of life on the way! Work hard for*
> *sin your whole life and your pension is death. But God's gift is*
> ***real life**, eternal life, delivered by Jesus, our Master.*
>
> Romans 6:20-23

1. Henri Nouwen, *Gracias! A Latin American Journal* (Maryknoll, New York: Orbis Books, 1993), 70.

V
Refocus

*It is absolutely clear that God has called you to a free
life. Just make sure that you don't use this freedom as an
excuse to do whatever you want to do and destroy your
freedom. Rather, use your freedom to serve one another in
love; that's how freedom grows. For everything we know
about God's Word is summed up in a single sentence:
Love others as you love yourself. That's an act of true freedom. If you bite and ravage each other, watch out—in no
time at all you will be annihilating each other, and where
will your precious freedom be then?*

*My counsel is this: Live freely, animated and motivated
by God's Spirit. Then you won't feed the compulsions of
selfishness. For there is a root of sinful self-interest in us
that is at odds with a free spirit, just as the free spirit is
incompatible with selfishness....*

Galatians 5:13-17

Turning our focus from ourselves to God is harder than we
think. The sweet freedom we gain from getting rid of selfishness and embracing Jesus in our hearts is life altering. As our
life begins to dial into Jesus in positive ways, we get stuck thinking
that we know what changes are necessary to align our hearts with
him. However, we repress the garbage layers that have accumulated
over the course of a lifetime.

It is obvious what kind of life develops out of trying to get your own way all the time: repetitive, loveless, cheap sex; a stinking accumulation of mental and emotional garbage; frenzied and joyless grabs for happiness; trinket gods; magic-show religion; paranoid loneliness; cutthroat competition; all-consuming-yet-never-satisfied wants; a brutal temper; an impotence to love or be loved; divided homes and divided lives; small-minded and lopsided pursuits; the vicious habit of depersonalizing everyone into a rival; uncontrolled and uncontrollable addictions; ugly parodies of community. I could go on....

Galatians 5:19-21

Our inclination is to deny that we are conducting ourselves in any of these selfish ways, but this is how serving *self* translates. Getting our own way, putting ourselves first in line, and justifying personal desires has become our way of life. Society wants us to believe that pleasing *self* is the path to life success. However, that path circles in the wrong direction; it goes opposite of the direction our Godly navigational tools point us to.

Thankfully, God reveals Himself to us even when we don't recognize we need Him or understand how to refocus our hearts on Him. He calls when we are confused and lost, when we are bruised and battered, and when we are totally self-focused. Sometimes we hear a faint whisper, but we are quickly distracted by the worries of the day and the noise of this world.

Remember, the world is constantly calling us to search for pyrite and enticing us to seek prestige, wealth, power and the relationships those bring. Each time we pick up a piece of pyrite, we take another trip around the island circle, enduring another cycle of discontent, anger and disappointment. Why do we do this? We are painfully unaware that our battered hearts are leading us to gather more pyrite, fool's gold that draws us deeper down the paths of destruction, creating layer upon layer of bruises and calluses and walls around our hearts.

The daily process of refocusing our hearts and connecting to Jesus as our Captain and the Holy Spirit as our Navigator will be different for each of us. Though we are uniquely made in God's image, each of us has a different backstory and different family dynamics. Our river journeys are never the same. There may be some similarities, but the reality is that each of us has our own set of behaviors and traits that we dragged into the boat after nearly drowning; we need to reckon with them as we set our compass on God's plan. But how do we deal with the bruises, calluses and walls of our past? How do we set our compass on God's plan for us? The "how" is always the question. There is never an easy answer.

One way is that of conviction. Some people describe it as a "gut" feeling. Conviction can be the realization that a thought process or outward action does or does not glorify God. In this process, we are focusing on convictions that address behaviors in our lives that need to be adjusted. For example, it can be the realization that a common behavioral trait in a family or habit is unhealthy and needs to be changed. Maybe it is the realization that the phrase, "this is just the way I am," is simply an excuse to behave badly. Maybe it is in the realization that the harsh tone in which we speak to our spouse or parent would never be used when speaking to someone else. It can be an awareness that we need to change what we enjoy listening to or watching. Conviction warns us when we are close to entering into behavior that will take our focus off God. Conviction also can make us aware of layers that surround our hearts.

Picture an onion. An onion is a smelly yet tasty vegetable and a great ingredient to liven up foods of all kinds. The structure of the onion includes a dry, papery, scaly outside with layers of meaty, moist onion inside. Each layer has a skin or membrane that wraps around it. Onions are actually "nutrient dense," meaning they are low in calories but high in nutrient content. They contain antioxidants and have other impressive health benefits. For some people, one uncomfortable side effect from ingesting onions is stomach upset. Of course, consuming onions gives you bad breath, and preparing onions makes you cry!

Now, let's picture ourselves as onions. Wait! Who wants to be an onion? Sure, there are health benefits, but that doesn't overcome the troubling side effects. We don't want to be onions. We want to be something sweet and lovely, like lettuce! Lettuce has layers, too—crisp, green leaves stacked in tantalizing freshness around a lovely heart. Lettuce is the main ingredient of most salads, is easy to prepare, and has no side effects in eating or preparation.

However, as we refocus on a new direction for our hearts during our river journey, our personal evaluation brings to light our reality. No lettuce here, friends. We are "stinkin' onions"! We are born a stinky and stubborn people. As we experience life, we develop layer upon layer of worldly behaviors and traits that produce bruises, calluses and walls around our hearts. At the same time this worldly layering is occurring, God also is layering knowledge of Him and His love. When God starts revealing these layers, He makes us aware of the heart changes that need to occur to move onward. "Onward" means that we recognize the layers, acknowledge the bruise, callus or wall, and determine that our hearts need to be healed.

Additionally, we need to understand that these layers come from childhood, teenage and adult experiences. The order of the layers is influenced by choices we make, choices others make that impact us, and worldly circumstances that we have no control over. The thickness of the layers can be impacted by parentless experiences, bad parenting or the opposite—parenting based on unconditional love. Some people will have layers that develop from physical illness, mental challenges or environmental circumstances. The layering also can be influenced by the misinterpretation of events or experiences as perceived wrongs as well as by accurate glimpses of truth and understanding.

As we refocus our hearts on God, these layers begin to be revealed, reworked, peeled, pruned and removed. How does that occur? Changes to the layers occur according to God's plan for our lives. For example, God can remove a layer instantaneously through love, grace and generosity. He also can rework or prune a layer using everyday situations. Of course, we can choose to cooperate or not. Our hate, jealousy or greed can expand an existing undesirable layer, making it more difficult to deal with. Unfortunately, healthy layers get squished between unhealthy layers, resulting in one big stinkin' onion.

To make it more interesting, we are all different stinkin' onions. What for some of us might be a flimsy outside layer that can be easily removed could be for someone else a thick, strong inner layer. Thick inner layers that have developed over a lifetime usually take more time and effort to remove. Additionally, the way God helps us work through our own onion layers is personal. As we sit with God and our onion layers, let's use Luke 6 as a beginning guiding signpost:

> *To you who are ready for the truth, I say this: Love your enemies. Let them bring out the best in you, not the worst. When someone gives you a hard time, respond with the energies of prayer for that person. If someone slaps you in the face, stand there and take it. If someone grabs your shirt, giftwrap your best coat and make a present of it. If someone takes unfair advantage of you, use the occasion to practice the servant life. No more tit-for-tat stuff. Live generously.*
>
> Luke 6:27-30

In order to love our enemy, we must recognize our need to forgive the offense and the offender. This happens through prayer, which is communicating with God. Is God asking us to move past ourselves and how we "feel" and onward towards loving the unlovable people in our lives?

> *Here is a simple rule of thumb for behavior: Ask yourself what you want people to do for you; then grab the initiative and do it for **them**!...*
>
> *I tell you, love your enemies. Help and give without expecting a return. You'll never—I promise—regret it! Live out this God-created identity the way our Father lives toward us, generously and graciously, even when we're at our worst. Our Father is kind; you be kind.*
>
> Luke 6:31, 35-36

Kindness based on God's direction produces different results than kindness based on our own desire to be loved and appreciated or to get ahead. Is God asking us to refocus our efforts on blessing people on His agenda and not necessarily those on ours?

> *Don't pick on people, jump on their failures, criticize their faults—unless, of course, you want the same treatment. Don't condemn those who are down; that hardness can boomerang. Be easy on people; you'll find life a lot easier. Give away your life; you'll find life given back, but not merely given back—given back with bonus and blessing. Giving, not getting, is the way. Generosity begets generosity.*
>
> Luke 6:37-38

Generosity based on God's direction furthers His Kingdom using resources He has provided. Our money, time and talents are actually His resources given to us to share as He directs. Our kind of generosity many times produces worldly satisfaction that is designed to promote ourselves. Is God challenging us to reevaluate why we are generous, how we are distributing His resources, and with whom we are sharing them?

> *He quoted a proverb: "'Can a blind man guide a blind man?' Wouldn't they both end up in the ditch? An apprentice doesn't lecture the master. The point is to be careful who you follow as your teacher."*
>
> Luke 6:39-40

God's wisdom is not the world's wisdom. Refocusing on God reorders our misplaced dependence on others. God should be first—ahead of spouses, parents, siblings, friends or even pastors and counselors. Is God challenging us to refocus our attention on Him and His wise counsel?

> *It's easy to see a smudge on your neighbor's face and be oblivious to the ugly sneer on your own. Do you have the nerve to say, "Let me wash your face for you," when your own face is distorted by contempt? It's this I-know-better-than-you mentality again, playing a holier-than-thou part*

instead of just living your own part. Wipe that ugly sneer off your own face and you might be fit to offer a washcloth to your neighbor.

Luke 6:41-42

Judgment of others is a nasty habit of many of us. It distracts us and closes us off from what God has for us in this day. It is a diversionary tactic of the evil one; it encourages us to open our mouths in ignorance instead of our hearts in prayer. God tells us that "kind mercy wins over harsh judgment every time" (James 2:13). Is God challenging us to refocus on carrying out His mercy instead of our judgment?

You don't get wormy apples off a healthy tree, nor good apples off a diseased tree. The health of the apple tells the health of the tree. You must begin with your own life-giving lives. It's who you are, not what you say and do, that counts. Your true being brims over into true words and deeds.

Luke 6:43-45

When we are pyrite gatherers, we display the diseased fruit within our hearts. When we refocus on God, we become His gold gatherers displaying His fruits as listed in Galatians 5:22-23—love, joy, peace, patience, kindness, goodness, gentleness, faithfulness and self-control. Is God challenging us to reorder our lives from within so that His fruit can be displayed to the world today?

Why are you so polite with me, always saying "Yes, sir," and "That's right, sir," but never doing a thing I tell you? These words I speak to you are not mere additions to your life, homeowner improvements to your standard of living. They are foundation words, words to build a life on.

Luke 6:46-47

God's Word is the foundation of freedom living. But many of us read or listen to His Word without ever applying it. Others of us fail to even crack open the manual to gain the insight needed to steer us onto the correct path. Is God challenging us to actually read His Word, seek its wisdom from Him, and apply it as He directs?

> *If you work the words into your life, you are like a smart car-*
> *penter who dug deep and laid the foundation of his house on*
> *bedrock. When the river burst its banks and crashed against*
> *the house, nothing could shake it; it was built to last. But if you*
> *just use my words in Bible studies and don't work them into*
> *your life, you are like a dumb carpenter who built a house but*
> *skipped the foundation. When the swollen river came crashing*
> *in, it collapsed like a house of cards. It was a total loss.*
>
> Luke 6:46-49

If we accept this truth, the layers start to be transformed. As we read the navigation manual and meditate on its verses, we need to ask God to help us evaluate the layers of our own onion. Maybe a layer needs to be revealed, peeled off, reordered, reworked or strengthened. Maybe a behavior of the past is no longer something that feels right to us even though it may be a perfectly satisfactory behavior for someone else. We must not look at our onions and decide what needs to go without consulting God, however. The key is to take one day at a time and focus on what God shows us in the particular day we are in. We need to ask God to refocus our hearts on Him, and He will bring the truth to light.

Our relationship with the Captain and the Navigator is essential to the health of our soul. The process of asking God to reveal the layers of our stinkin' onions and refocusing on Jesus for the repair work heals our hearts and strengthens us for the journey yet to come. Remember, this exposure of our onion layers is a lifelong process. It is God's way of refocusing us on Him. In transforming the layers of our stinkin' onions, God is refocusing us through trusting in Him and obeying His direction even when we don't know the why, how or when. The free life equals trusting and obeying God.

> *Once when he was standing on the shore of Lake Gen-*
> *nesaret, the crowd was pushing in on him to better hear the*
> *Word of God. He noticed two boats tied up. The fishermen*
> *had just left them and were out scrubbing their nets. He*

climbed into the boat that was Simon's and asked him to put out a little from the shore. Sitting there, using the boat for a pulpit, he taught the crowd.

When he finished teaching, he said to Simon, "Push out into deep water and let your nets out for a catch."

Simon said, "Master, we've been fishing hard all night and haven't caught even a minnow. But if you say so, I'll let out the nets." It was no sooner said than done—a huge haul of fish, straining the nets past capacity. They waved to their partners in the other boat to come help them. They filled both boats, nearly swamping them with the catch.

Simon Peter, when he saw it, fell to his knees before Jesus. "Master, leave. I'm a sinner and can't handle this holiness. Leave me to myself." When they pulled in that catch of fish, awe over-whelmed Simon and everyone with him. It was the same with James and John, Zebedee's sons, coworkers with Simon.

Jesus said to Simon, "There is nothing to fear. From now on you'll be fishing for men and women." They pulled their boats up on the beach, left them, nets and all, and followed him.

Luke 5:1-11

God has embedded within us a yearning for a relationship with Him. We are distracted from that relationship because we trust ourselves more than we trust Jesus. Even with Jesus in our boat, we still doubt the power of His presence. The disciples knew there were no fish because they had been fishing all night. Jesus told them to go fishing anyway. Why? Because He wanted them to know that with Him in their boat, all things are possible. They obeyed without being fully confident that they would catch anything. The result was a blessing more than they could hope for or imagine. They received the blessing because they put their trust in Jesus over their trust in their own knowledge.

∿ ROBIN'S JOURNEY

I was at a point in my river journey where I was trying to walk in step with Jesus but was not always successful. I was enthusiastically His, but sometimes that meant that I jumped ahead of Him in my quest to serve Him. I believe this is a common issue with beginning Christians. We leap ahead on our own and determine what we should be doing instead of listening for His direction and relying on His timing.

My girls were almost four and five years old. We yearned for more children, hopefully a son to complement our lovely girls. However, I was resigned to the fact that we probably would have no more children. I mean, it had been three and a half years of trying since we were blessed with Rachael. With our history, I was a realist! It seemed like it was just not going to happen.

It was a lovely, March Sunday when, as always, Pastor Pat had a sermon seemingly just for me called "Spring Cleaning." She spoke of our need to faithfully utilize the resources God has provided to us and, when those resources were not of use to us anymore, to pass them on to someone else. This is how God's Kingdom blossoms and expands— by Christians sharing with others the love they have received. It was a lesson in good stewardship.

As it usually did, her sermon struck me at my core. I realized that I was hording our children's stuff in anticipation of another baby. Obviously, that was not happening! After sitting with God and praying about my response, I spent the next week boxing up all the baby clothing and paraphernalia, from swings to car seats to all the infant toys. It was embarrassing how much stuff we had. I tried to get the crib down from the attic, but that was just too much because we had one of those pull-down ladders that required several people to maneuver things down it!

It was with mixed feelings that I donated the items to a local charity. Although I had donated before, it seemed to me that this was new. In the past I had donated out of my excess monies or things I did not want. This time, I donated out of my recognition that God wanted me to give away the items I was hoarding, even if I might need them again. As I gave them away, it seemed like I was giving away my hope of another child; at the same time, I realized what blessings God had bestowed upon me with the two girls I had. His provision for me was not only sufficient but also over the top. I was sure that many families would benefit from the ripple effect of the blessings we received and then passed on.

You have probably already guessed what happened! I did indeed become pregnant the next month. Would I have become pregnant regardless of my obedience to give away all the stuff? Possibly, but the answer is irrelevant. I do know this: I would not have appreciated the miracle as much had I been disobedient. Furthermore, when I was eight months into my pregnancy, we unexpectedly moved. My obedience saved me from packing up and schlepping all that stuff to our new house!

God blessed us with our son, Sam, and provided us with all that we needed to take care of him. As time passed, I was not led to give away all of Sam's baby stuff. Why? Because we needed them for another indescribable blessing: his brother and our son, Andy!

This particular series of events was a "how to live the free life" lesson for me. Remember, freedom equals trust. I actually got it right on that day by listening to His gold gatherer, consulting with Him about the wisdom she passed on, and acting upon His direction. Even though I did not want to give away the baby items, I did it anyway, trusting that someone else would be blessed in the process and not expecting anything in return. I also learned that the wisdom that I received was not necessarily the wisdom received by others who had heard the same sermon. Our obedience is not someone else's obedience, which is why it is so important to stay out of other people's journeys unless we are called to intercede.

Many layers of my stinkin' onion were transformed during the years when my kids were young. As previously mentioned, I jumped in front of God many times in my quest to be useful to Him. I had "the need to be useful" piece of pyrite in my backpack. God patiently reworked that onion layer, teaching me that "my usefulness" was not in my useful service to Him but instead in my obedience, trust and faithfulness to Him.

Those years also brought to light another onion layer comprised of beautiful specks of pyrite and identified as my desire to get everything right. My "perfection" layer needed strong reworking and much trimming to rein in my overachieving self that was set on doing things "right." In essence, I wanted my own way not only for myself but also for others. This need brought about much discord and many challenges as I tried to keep my order with four children and a husband who did not give in to my perfectionism. Without his strong spirit and notable sense of humor, we would not have survived. Iron does sharpen iron, as Proverbs says!

When we refocus our hearts on God, He communicates with us through acts of obedience and trust. He tailors His response specifically to each of us individually. Like Robin's sermon experience and Tara's moms' group experience recounted in the previous chapter, God communicates in countless ways, as if catching our attention and winking at us. A "God wink" could be a song that is played on the radio at just the right time or a person God places in our path at just the right moment. It could be a joyful reminder of an event with our deceased mother or the smell of our favorite childhood meal. It could be a rainbow that appears at the moment we doubt He will come through with a plan or an eagle soaring ahead of us when we think His plans are not coming to fruition. It could be audible or perceived in our hearts. "God winks" are instances that help us realize how special we are to God because the signal was for our hearts alone.

We often miss Godly communication because our focus is on ourselves instead of on God. Unfortunately, our failure to keep focused results in missing the guidance of the signposts. The guidance of the signposts, if discerned, can prevent "stinkin' thinkin'" by guiding our thoughts towards God. When we are focused on God and seeking communication with Him, worries begin to fade. We begin to realize that worry is a lack of trust in Him. The more time we spend with Him, the more we trust Him. The more we trust Him, the more we realize that He will never leave us or forsake us (see Hebrews 13:5). In that realization, we comprehend the freedom we have in Him. That freedom translates to peace in our souls.

But what happens when we live God's way? He brings gifts into our lives, much the same way that fruit appears in an orchard—things like affection for others, exuberance about life, serenity. We develop a willingness to stick with things, a sense of compassion in the heart, and a conviction that a basic holiness permeates things and people. We find ourselves involved in loyal commitments, not needing to force our way in life, able to marshal and direct our energies wisely.

Legalism is helpless in bringing this about; it only gets in the way. Among those who belong to Christ, everything connected with getting our own way and mindlessly responding to what everyone else calls necessities is killed off for good—crucified.

Since this is the kind of life we have chosen, the life of the Spirit, let us make sure that we do not just hold it as an idea in our heads or a sentiment in our hearts, but work out its implications in every detail of our lives. That means we will not compare ourselves with each other as if one of us were better and another worse. We have far more interesting things to do with our lives. Each of us is an original.

Galatians 5:22-26

Original. Unique. Exclusive. Special. The plan God has designed for our lives will prosper us and prosper others through us. Through recognizing His communication with us, we see His goodness; we see His kindness. We begin to realize the truth of the words the prophet Jeremiah shared from God: "'For I know the plans I have for you,' declares the LORD, 'plans to prosper you and not to harm you, plans to give you hope and a future'" (Jeremiah 29:11 NIV).

We also see His discipline and His power. We see His hand in our circumstances and begin to recognize that the challenges we are given, He allowed to occur. Our job is to stick with Him through seeking His presence in all situations. A seeking soul always will be filled, but if we don't seek, we can't find His plan. His plan for us is specifically for us alone to complete; it is pointless to compare our plan with someone else's.

How do we know we are following His plan for our lives and not just making ethical or moral decisions? Ethical and moral decisions will help us sleep well at night and keep our conscience clear, but the main motivator is self-satisfaction. Being overly pleased with one's self is an indicator of wrong motivation. Following God's plan means constant reconnection with the source of our strength: God.

God's plans will always involve planting a seed and producing fruit. The seeds He plants will come in our communing with Him and by following His guidance. The fruits we produce are referred to as the fruits of the Spirit: love, joy, peace, patience, kindness, goodness, faithfulness and self-control. The entirety of His Kingdom is strengthened by these types of fruits ripening and being shared in a mature harvest.

How does His seed become a ripened fruit? Growth and change! The growth process God guides each of us through can look vastly different from the growth process in another person, even when yielding the same type of fruit. Not only can it look different, but it also can be accomplished at different speeds! It is in these everyday changes that we as individuals can cooperate with His plan.

Jesus taught:

> *Don't look for shortcuts to God. The market is flooded with surefire, easygoing formulas for a successful life that can be practiced in your spare time. Don't fall for that stuff, even though crowds of people do. The way to life—to God!—is vigorous and requires total attention.*
>
> Matthew 7:13-14

VI
Rebuild

At the point in our river journey when we realize that we believe in God, Jesus and the Holy Spirit and recognize our need for God, we begin the process of turning from our rebellion to focusing on Him and rebuilding our broken lives based on His direction. The peeling off or reworking of the layers around our hearts reveals the brokenness within our souls. This brokenness is what attempts to pull us back down into the deep as our Captain patiently instructs us from His place at the helm.

The process of rebuilding is an ongoing, lifelong process. It took many of us decades to get to where we are on the Isle of I. Although our Captain can remove us quickly from any situation, it is usually a long and slow process to peel back the layers that have been built up over years of dedication to self. It takes focused work on our part as well as a commitment to build our relationship with Jesus to heal much of our brokenness.

The daily process of rebuilding may be exhausting and taxing at times, but it is also exhilarating. We will make mistakes, but we also will learn to immediately give those instances to God. Fortunately, when we recognize our errors, God is able to redeem any situation for His glory. Seeing the movement of God uplifts us from our focus on failure to refocusing on Him. The end result is the rebuilding of our inner brokenness into a new level of maturity.

Paul explains it this way in his letter to the Romans:

So here's what I want you to do, God helping you: Take your everyday, ordinary life—your sleeping, eating, going-to-work,

and walking-around life—and place it before God as an
offering. Embracing what God does for you is the best thing
you can do for him. Don't become so well-adjusted to your
culture that you fit into it without even thinking. Instead, fix
your attention on God. You'll be changed from the inside
out. Readily recognize what he wants from you, and quickly
respond to it. Unlike the culture around you, always dragging
you down to its level of immaturity, God brings the best out
of you, develops well-formed maturity in you.

Romans 12:1-2

God provides us with many tools, starting with His saving grace, His right relationship with us, and His truths, as well as the fruits of the Spirit—love, joy, peace, patience, kindness, goodness, faithfulness, gentleness and self-control. All these tools assist us not only in maturing and thriving in His Kingdom, but also in turning and staying away from our bad habits. Our tendency is to rely on our own initiative and resolution to steer ourselves clear from repeatedly falling into these familiar traps. However, the truth is we are drawn to certain behaviors that test our resolve. We all have stinkin' onion layers. It is vital to know what our individual trials are so that we do not hinder or delay the rebuilding effort. Using God's tools and combat strategies will prepare us for the challenges ahead. Here are a few that have worked for us.

Our first strategy is to recognize that today is a good day to begin. The past is over; the future is not yet here. Our job is to do what needs to be done in the day we are in. God has given us this day—"today" must not be wasted with excuses. We have been given enough strength for the challenges of today. Tomorrow has worries of its own, and God will provide strength to battle those issues tomorrow. Today we focus on today.

Give your entire attention to what God is doing right now,
and don't get worked up about what may or may not hap-
pen tomorrow. God will help you deal with whatever hard
things come up when the time comes.

Matthew 6:34

Gear up for combat! Excuses, worries and belief that we don't have enough strength—these will drag us down into a bog and result in a failure to start today. If we don't start today, the challenges that we face will seem insurmountable and cause us to sink into the bog. Starting today puts us on a new and right path according to God's plan.

A second strategy is to turn to our Captain and read and meditate on the words that He has given to us. We can read the Bible, our manual, in print or online or through an app on our phones. We can listen to it while we drive or jog or sit alone. We can examine His Word through a Bible study or online teaching. Abundant daily reading programs and devotions are available. Countless books and references can help us interpret and understand the meaning of each and every verse:

> There's nothing like the written Word of God for showing you the way to salvation through faith in Christ Jesus. Every part of Scripture is God-breathed and useful one way or another—showing us truth, exposing our rebellion, correcting our mistakes, training us to live God's way. Through the Word we are put together and shaped up for the tasks God has for us.
>
> 2 Timothy 3:15-17

When we read, meditate and speak His words out loud, we can expect not only action, but also unexpected occurrences. Our eyes should be open and our hearts expectant to receive and observe how Jesus will move in our "today." We need to conscientiously take in what God places on our hearts in any moment, whether that message comes by a God wink a conviction or some other means of communication.

Gear up for combat! When we do not set aside daily time to read or listen to His living Word, we bypass the guidance these Scriptures could provide. Without awareness of the purpose of the guiding signposts, we stumble onward with only ourselves as captain and navigator. We, in essence, ignore the instruction of the Holy Spirit. The good news is that our Captain can catch our attention through His design every moment of every day.

So, let's just start now. Jesus asks:

Are you tired? Worn out? Burned out on religion? Come to me. Get away with me and you'll recover your life. I'll show you how to take a real rest. Walk with me and work with me—watch how I do it. Learn the unforced rhythms of grace. I won't lay anything heavy or ill-fitting on you. Keep company with me and you'll learn to live freely and lightly.
Matthew 11:28-30

A third combat strategy is to pick a program that fits our current lifestyle and enables us to start today. For instance, remember "John Wesley's Great Experiment," the experiment with a new way of living mentioned in chapter III? It involved getting up early in order to have time to read Scripture and meditate on it. The reading and meditation resulted in doing something kind for someone each day and journaling, as well as weekly tithing and sharing the experience with others. Whatever program we choose, it should help us rebuild what God has pointed us towards during our day-to-day life.

And when you come before God, don't turn that into a theatrical production either. All these people making a regular show out of their prayers, hoping for stardom! Do you think God sits in a box seat?

Here's what I want you to do: Find a quiet, secluded place so you won't be tempted to role-play before God. Just be there as simply and honestly as you can manage. The focus will shift from you to God, and you will begin to sense his grace.
Matthew 6:5-6

Gear up for combat! Fully commit to a God-centered plan. We might have to get up earlier, go to bed earlier or skip our Facebook session after dinner in order to make time for God. If we are able to commit to God in these simple ways, then He will open our eyes and ears. These daily disciplines should not be viewed as mandatory rules for living but as tools to remind us to constantly focus on God, who is rebuilding and reworking our lives each day.

Implementing these strategies will cause change in our lives. *Get ready!*

We need to set our compass on a new attitude about change, similar to how a familiar character in a much-loved children's series, *The Chronicles of Narnia* by C. S. Lewis, did. Lucy Pevensie is the youngest of the Pevensie children. She is a sweet, honest, innocent, eight-year-old child when she takes her first step through the wardrobe into Narnia in *The Lion, the Witch and the Wardrobe*. Lucy is the original finder and explorer of Narnia, and, as only a child can do, she simply sees wonderment in Narnia and doesn't doubt or disbelieve. She doesn't ask *why* she is out of the wardrobe; she doesn't spend too much time wondering *why* it is now winter or *why* she meets a talking faun. Lucy takes everything at face value. She was in the wardrobe; now she is not. She is transported to a magical place and, with no inhibitions and no fear, smiles and resoundingly agrees to tea with Mr. Tumnus.

How often do we step into a new environment with the same attitude as Lucy? Usually, in a new situation, the best attitude we can muster is hopeful curiosity. Realities of adulthood cause us to be cautious and calculating. We look for explanations and probable cause. Frankly, we are generally skeptical and tend towards faultfinding. This adult tendency makes it much harder to change our attitudes. We find it easier to continue in the same established patterns even if they are not the best for us. The false sense of security these patterns promote can debilitate us into thinking we are safe in the midst of a raging river.

As we rebuild, we implement new strategies with a new attitude towards change. This will fortify the temple Jesus is building in our lives to serve Him better. Jesus rebuilds by loving us forever and always. Even when we are not heeding Him, He is cheering for us through the learning and changing process and is our greatest encourager. He knows it will take us numerous times to learn the life lessons He has for us. His unique, sweet love comes to us free of disappointment as well as with full knowledge of our every failure. The good thing is that when we choose Jesus as our Captain, we can be assured that the rebuilding effort is moving us from standing in precarious waters or being abandoned on an unknown path to a life standing on a solid rock foundation. Change just takes a rebuilding effort that is directed by our Captain and carried out by us through the prompting of the Holy Spirit.

> Or, to put it another way, you are God's house. Using the gift God gave me as a good architect, I designed blue-prints; Apollos is putting up the walls. Let each carpenter who comes on the job take care to build on the foundation! Remember, there is only one foundation, the one already laid: Jesus Christ. Take particular care in picking out your building materials. Eventually there is going to be an inspection. If you use cheap or inferior materials, you'll be found out. The inspection will be thorough and rigorous. You won't get by with a thing. If your work passes inspection, fine; if it doesn't, your part of the building will be torn out and started over. But **you** won't be torn out; you'll survive—but just barely.
>
> You realize, don't you, that you are the temple of God, and God himself is present in you? No one will get by with vandalizing God's temple, you can be sure of that. God's temple is sacred—and you, remember, **are** the temple.
>
> 1 Corinthians 3:9-17

⌣ TARA'S JOURNEY

About ten years ago, Mike and I moved our family from a small city closer to our childhood home in rural Pennsylvania. Mike decided on a job change, and it was fortunate that the move would bring us closer to our families. What was unfortunate was that we had to move three full floors of belongings, two adults, three children and a cat.

How do people acquire such a large houseful of belongings in only eight years of marriage? The answer: inexperience and space. We were inexperienced in understanding that accumulated stuff has to have a reckoning day. Because we had extra space, we just did not know how to politely say "no" to storage of others' belongings. Mike and I lost our grandparents in a matter of a few short years, leaving three households of memorabilia to sort through and clean out. The things that weren't particularly precious to anyone came to live in our extra rooms and attic.

Early on in the move, we became overwhelmed with the amount of items we had acquired. The sort-and-separate tactic used before packing was insurmountable. Mike and I are both type-A personalities and work best from spreadsheets and outlook calendars. Call it what you like, but the term *Excel* in our home is used in a loving fashion. So, after careful review, the decision was made to not waste time sorting while trying to move. Everything would come to live in our new garage. We set a rule that each box would be categorized and cataloged before it entered our new home to help pare down from our extreme excess. We identified the task, created a plan and began the process.

Enter the Lord with a rebuilding project to repair a structural crack in Tara's foundation! This is how I remember the conversation of a particular Saturday transpiring.

Me: "What is on your agenda for today, babe?"

Mike: "Well, I'd like to take the encyclopedias to the basement and…blah, blah, blah."

Not a very long conversation, right? Actually, it didn't end there. Mike's lips were still moving, but I was done listening. There was a much more intense conversation going on in my head between me, myself and I. Here's how it sounded in my head:

> "WHAT in the WORLD?! I am sick of being a pack mule!! I refuse to carry those ridiculous encyclopedias to the basement.
>
> "DID YOU FORGET HOW MUCH LUGGING I DID DURING OUR MOVE? ALL OF IT! Yes, up and down three stories carrying useless stuff.
>
> "Sure, you took care of the garage, BUT WHO ARE WE KIDDING? The contents of that garage could have gone up in smoke, and we would never have missed a thing.

"I AM NOT moving those encyclopedias. Who even keeps encyclopedias anymore? There are three heavy boxes! NO WAY. NOT ON YOUR LIFE. I'M NOT DOING IT."

Holy cow! Such an intense and powerful conversation, *all by myself, inside my head*, complete with capital letters! Looking back, I think I was shouting inside my head. How else could I have missed the Lord's voice? I was so focused on my fierce reaction to Mike's simple statement that I had no clue what was about to happen.

The problem with any conversation, especially an angry conversation in your head, is that it is totally one-sided. What is critical to remember in this story is that Mike *never* asked me to move the encyclopedias. He simply responded to the question I posed and told me about his agenda for the day.

I leaped to the conclusion that he was implying that moving the books should be on my agenda. For a task that I was never invited to participate in, I was surely determined *not* to do it or to help in any way. After the shouting in my head ceased, I was able to converse out of my mouth again. The rest of that Saturday went on, and you can be assured that I was not found anywhere near the garage.

As the following Saturday approached, our agendas were reviewed—and the encyclopedias were still on Mike's agenda. *I*, a very capital I, still wasn't moving those *out-of-date, ridiculously heavy* books; nor was I, a very lowercase i, being asked to by my husband. At that very moment, a thought quietly sneaked into my consciousness and pointed out that Mike technically hadn't asked me for my help. But if he should actually say those words, I was prepared for him. My ammunition was at the ready; my tongue was primed for action.

These words of wisdom from Psalm 141:3 were not in my forethoughts: "Post a guard at my mouth, GOD, set a watch at the door of my lips." I was ready to inventory all the work I had been tallying during the move. This catalog of work consisted of comparisons of the work I had physically completed versus the work Mike had physically completed. You feel worried for me, don't you? You know I'm treading on dangerous ground with this selfish, foolhardy, incorrect comparison chart. I'm cringing along with you as you contemplate this scene. Never fear! The Lord was there to rescue me.

The Lord said, "Move the books."

I remember thinking, "I did *not* just hear that," yet it was a quiet, firm request.

"Move the books."

Now why in the *world* would the Lord need to get into this conversation? There are many things He could be concerned with other than this book matter.

"Why does it matter to You, Lord, if I move the books or not? Let me show You *my* list, Lord. My list shows how much more physical work I do than Mike. You must have forgotten how hard I've worked. I've already moved *so many* items in this relocation, and those encyclopedias aren't *even useful*! I *don't* understand why You are butting in, and *no*, I am not moving those books."

"Move the books."

These words were the Lord's message to me consistently over the next three to four weeks. Repeatedly, I'd hear, *"Move the books."* I'd counter with a civil, "No, I'm not moving the books." The conversation reminded me of the old fairy tale "The Little Red Hen."

> *"Who will move these books?"* said the Lord.
> "Not I," said Tara.

The Lord is ever loving and tenacious. Finally, after approximately five weeks of arguing with the Lord—*me being the only one actually arguing*—I gave in. It was a midweek day when I conceded. Any thoughts connecting Mike with these books had long since faded. This matter of my will was between the Lord and me.

Defeated, I said, "Okay, Lord. I don't know why it is so important to You that I move these boxes of useless encyclopedias, but I will. I will move these books out of the garage, down the hill and to the basement. I'll do it for You. I don't care about my comparison chart or these nasty books anymore. If this is what You want from me, then so be it. I'll move the books. But please, I just don't want to talk about it anymore."

I moved those three oversized boxes of heavy encyclopedias out of the garage, down the hill and into the basement. It was done. The conversation was over, and I breathed a sigh of relief. Being at odds with the Lord is exhausting.

Mike came home from work that very day and was extremely excited as he entered the house. "Babe! Babe! Did you move those heavy boxes of books?" There was a short comment in my head, *Yes, I moved those stupid books.* However, out loud I replied nonchalantly, "Yeah?"

He scooped me up and gave me such a squeeze! "Thank you so much! Those books have been clogging up my agenda and have been on my mind for weeks! I just couldn't get to them. They were so heavy! How did you get them down the hill? Thank you so much for thinking of me."

I'm pretty sure when he said the "thinking of me" part, my heart was squeezed so hard that it screamed. It was much louder than my earlier shouting conversation and truly painful to hear. Good grief! It had taken the better part of five weeks to get this stubborn woman to learn how to think of others before herself! My list-making, self-righteous, self-talk nonsense and my downright refusal to complete a task the Lord set before me had prevented peace in my husband's mind for over a month. I was so busy putting myself first and compiling my list that I never stopped to consider Mike. My need for my comparison chart to be justified coupled with my need for recognition coupled with my *need* to be *right* blotted out and overruled any other thoughts.

> *Love cares more for others than for self.*
> *Love doesn't want what it doesn't have.*
> *Love doesn't strut,*
> *Doesn't have a swelled head,*
> *...Isn't always "me first,"*
> *...Doesn't keep score of the sins of others...*
> 1 Corinthians 13:4-5

I sorely missed the mark as I sat alone on the Isle of I. I failed to use any combat strategies or tools in my toolbox; I failed to recognize any guiding signposts along my five-week path of disobedience. The obvious conclusion to this embarrassing story is that the Lord often uses simple life experiences to get us to pay closer attention to Him. Did it matter to the Lord where we stored our useless encyclopedias? I don't think so. Did it matter to the Lord that I obey Him? Absolutely. Do we have to understand why He asks us to behave in a certain way? Not necessarily.

He desires our obedience in all matters ranging from what we believe to be important to what we believe to be insignificant. When we are obedient, He can use our behaviors and actions to reach people for the Kingdom. Slowly, the Lord is rebuilding me, teaching me day by day how to listen, see and behave in a way that glorifies Him. My river journey is ever changing and often unexpected. It is new each day. And there is freedom in not being in charge while safely journeying with my Captain.

> *"I don't think the way you think.*
> *The way you work isn't the way I work."*
>
> Gᴏᴅ's *Decree.*
> *"For as the sky soars high above earth,*
> *so the way I work surpasses the way you work,*
> *and the way I think is beyond the way you think."*
> Isaiah 55:8-9

God's way of rebuilding each of us is in the only way He can—His way. We have no idea how that will happen, but our attitude going into each new day will set the stage for our success. Are we preparing for our day using the strategies and tools He has provided? Are we expectantly looking for how God is working in our today and cooperating with Him?

Let's visit with Jesus as He teaches His disciples another foundational lesson:

> *One day when large groups of people were walking along*
> *with him, Jesus turned and told them, "Anyone who comes*

*to me but refuses to let go of father, mother, spouse, chil-
dren, brothers, sisters—yes, even one's own self!—can't be
my disciple. Anyone who won't shoulder his own cross and
follow behind me can't be my disciple.*

*"Is there anyone here who, planning to build a new house,
doesn't first sit down and figure the cost so you'll know if
you can complete it? If you only get the foundation laid and
then run out of money, you're going to look pretty foolish.
Everyone passing by will poke fun at you: 'He started something he couldn't finish.'*

*"Or can you imagine a king going into battle against another
king without first deciding whether it is possible with his ten
thousand troops to face the twenty thousand troops of the
other? And if he decides he can't, won't he send an emis-
sary and work out a truce?*

*"Simply put, if you're not willing to take what is dearest to
you, whether plans or people, and kiss it good-bye, you
can't be my disciple."*

Luke 14:25-33

Jesus is telling us here that He needs to be first in our lives before
anything or anybody else. We need to turn our attention fully to Him
in order for Him to rebuild our lives. He has to be our foundation. We
will have important, life-altering questions that don't get answered at
first; we want to know the answers before we think we can embark on
this "faith" journey. But we can't let those questions stop us. We will
learn as we go. The key is to "*go*" with the right attitude.

God has given us His manual as well as strategies and navigational
tools to assist us in this "go" process. As He works in our lives, we are
able to allow the Captain of our boat to be in charge. We begin to look
for the Holy Spirit and cooperate in His leading.

Rebuilding is a cycle of learning to listen, see and obediently refocus on God and the truths that Jesus teaches us. The purpose of

rebuilding is to allow God to heal our broken hearts. "This, in a nut-shell, is [God's] will: that everything handed over to me [Jesus] by the Father be completed—not a single detail missed—and at the wrap-up of time I have everything and everyone put together, upright and whole" (John 6:39). Jesus is about rebuilding and putting us together, upright and whole. The way that is done is for us to follow Him moment by moment up and until we take our final breath.

VII

Renew

Make Insight Your Priority
Good friend, take to heart what I'm telling you;
collect my counsels and guard them with your life.
Tune your ears to the world of Wisdom;
set your heart on a life of Understanding.
That's right—if you make Insight your priority,
and won't take no for an answer,
Searching for it like a prospector panning for gold,
like an adventurer on a treasure hunt,
Believe me, before you know it Fear-of-GOD will be yours;
you'll have come upon the Knowledge of God.
And here's why: GOD gives out Wisdom free,
is plainspoken in Knowledge and Understanding.
He's a rich mine of Common Sense for those who live well,
a personal bodyguard to the candid and sincere.
He keeps his eye on all who live honestly,
and pays special attention to his loyally committed ones.
                                                    Proverbs 2:1-8

As Jesus works to stand us upright on a firm foundation in a moment-by-moment process, we need to actively participate! There is freedom in following the true Captain. We begin to see, hear and behave in a way that invites God into our everyday life. It is not that He wasn't there before; it is just that now we are seeing and hearing Him; we are tapping into His wisdom. We are recognizing "insight," which allows us to turn from our wayward ways towards Him. This change promotes a new pattern of living.

The key is to recognize when we are following God's wisdom instead of our own. If it is our own, we will take another trip around the circle. "Following" is an intentional act on our part to observe and seek the movement of God. As our day unfolds, we can utilize wisdom gained through our combat strategies and tools to compare what we are seeing, saying and participating in with what Jesus would do in those same circumstances.

To make this course of action easier to visualize, let's return to our school days and science fair projects. If you recall, a science experiment uses a control group to compare different variables. The control group never changes. Data is collected, analyzed and compared with the control group, and conclusions are formulated from those results.

God, Jesus and the Holy Spirit are our control group. They and Their promises are eternally constant. God is love (see 1 John 4:8). Jesus is God's love in human form. The Holy Spirit is God's love with us in this moment. God promises to never leave us or forsake us (see Hebrews 13:5). God is good (see Mark 10:18). He is always for us, never against us (see Romans 8:31). We find these and more of God's truths in His living Word. The Bible was written for us and is our constant data.

Similar to the scientific method, we can use our control group data to compare with the variables we encounter in our day. Some variables seem very inconsequential, like what color to paint our closet, while other variables are of major importance, like what career path to take. What we experience in our everyday lives are the variables. Our lives are in constant motion. Our environment, our jobs, our health, and our circle of family, friends, coworkers and acquaintances all change moment by moment.

When we compare the choices we make in our everyday lives against what Jesus would do in those same circumstances, data is collected. It is from this data that we arrive at conclusions that can be used to gauge if we are following God's wisdom and His path. God's path is filled with gold nuggets that are within His will and found in His way. They are obtained by cooperating with God in our daily walk and found as we seek God and cling to His unending love. Think back to when God's gold nuggets were in your grasp, but you failed to recognize them. All of us have mistakenly allowed our control group to be worldly successes or societal goals. But these successes and goals bring temporary satisfaction at best and have no lasting foundation. They are pyrite.

By using God's truth, wisdom and insight, we gain strength to navigate through circumstances that are outside of our control, yet within His. We can learn from Jesus to love deeply, knowing He loves us even more. We can cope with inevitable heartache knowing that the Holy Spirit will comfort us. We can turn from destructive behaviors knowing that when we seek God, we gain insight. We can change course and take a new approach to the question of which gold nugget to grasp, knowing our God gives wisdom abundantly.

> *Listen to good advice if you want to live well,*
> *an honored guest among wise men and women.*
> *An undisciplined, self-willed life is puny;*
> *an obedient, God-willed life is spacious.*
> *Fear-of-God is a school in skilled living—*
> *first you learn humility, then you experience glory.*
>
> Proverbs 15:31-33

When we view our constants in light of our variables, we end up with an evaluation method that is dependable and reliable: *refocus* on Jesus; *expect change* to happen; *accept* His timing; and *flourish* in freedom. Refocusing is dialing in to Jesus as our constant. We started this evaluation process when we recognized our need for God, turned from our rebellion and refocused our hearts on Jesus. Our onion layers are in the process of being rebuilt. Now, it is time to *expect change*!

Let's face it, most of us are not good at "change"; it is a "bad" word for many. We tend to want to cuddle in our comfort. We reach a "safe" place in the raging waters of life and just want to stay there on our secure island—not because we are safe, but because we think we are on a solid rock when we are actually on sinking sand. We can't go back, but we are too scared to go forward into the unknown.

Change is hard for many of us because we fear what we do not know. We are concentrating on our own self-preservation instead of seeking God's counsel. We are clutching this world's pyrite, which falsely secures us in the comfortable mess of our lives. Not only do we fear change, but we also fear the interruption of routine. Routines make us comfortable because they provide controlled stability. The problem is, when we become rigid and overly-attached to our routines, it results in the loss of flexibility. Flexibility is needed to operate under God's direction.

We all have routines on the surface of our lives as well as those that are hidden deeper. For example, a surface routine could be how we fold our towels. Does folding our towels have an impact on God's plan for us? Who is to say? We don't know. What we do know is this: we must recognize that a routine for one person may draw that person to God, but the exact same routine in another person may draw that individual away from God. Comparisons with others never work in this process. Such a comparison can falsely anchor us in an unproductive routine.

A hidden routine could be embedded within our personalities. Some of us are stuck in the routine of self-centered drama. What would we do if we didn't talk about all the bad things that are happening to us? We don't realize how our conversation constantly centers on self, and it is boring to those listening. When we actually hit a "lull" from the drama in our lives or realize no one is listening, we don't know how to act. The result is that we stir up more drama and ultimately get embroiled in a new sticky situation that refocuses us on ourselves.

Other hidden routines could be what we consider great comforts in our lives. Comforts can be rewards or "feel good" behaviors. Some examples of comfort routines are a nightly snack, "happy hour," cozy blankets, binge-watching television shows, social media surfing or online shopping. The examples are endless. The question is not whether the comfort routine is right or wrong, but whether the routine is preventing us from seeking and finding our comfort in Jesus.

Comfortable routines can cause stagnation, laziness and immobilization. They trap us in mediocrity, where we are neither hot nor cold but are just plain dull. They veil the pyrite weighing us down and suck the life out of us. When we are stuck in the bog of routine or comfort, we usually have sunk to the point where it is not easy for us to free ourselves. The wonderful conclusion of this examination into our routines and comforts is that we can relinquish control to the Captain. It is not for us to choose the path of how to come out of the bog, but to rely on God to show us the path. God carefully will reveal how to turn our time in the bog into something that is useful for navigation in this life.

Holding on to these comfortable routines is in opposition to God's path for us, which is to expect change. By trying to stay in the same routines or comforts, we are trying to make our lives be our control group. Impossible! When we joyfully release control of our moment-by-moment living to Jesus, we can view change as something that is expected and anticipated. The reality of things changing can be God's new and improved routine and comfort for us!

> *Give your entire attention to what God is doing right now, and don't get worked up about what may or may not happen tomorrow. God will help you deal with whatever hard things come up when the time comes.*
>
> Matthew 6:34

Throw up your hands and repeat these words: "*I don't know!*"

Usually the phrase, *I don't know*, is not a positive one. It is a phrase that comes with trepidation and uncertainty. It brings about feelings of inadequacy and unpreparedness. But let's *change* those feelings about this phrase by turning to our control group. We don't know what God's plan is because His ways are higher than our ways; His thoughts are beyond our thoughts (see Isaiah 55:8-9). He is only good. When "I don't know" is said with confidence that God does know, it becomes easier to *accept* God's timing.

The idea of accepting God's timing has never occurred to many of us because it is an underlying component to relinquishing control to God. We acknowledge that God is in control, but we want everything to fit into our own time frame. This cycle of thinking is another veiled mode of control—one that prevents us from fully trusting God. We want what we want when we want it.

Eventually, we begin to trust God's timing, but it takes awhile to get to that point in our journey. God can change anything in an instant, but most often He takes time to reorder our circumstances, rework our souls from within, and reconnect the dots. God's timing is perfection. When we accept that we "don't know" but trust that God does, we are free to live our everyday lives in His love. We begin to recognize that there is a purpose behind every circumstance of our day. These events are not random and disordered. God allows things to happen, both good and bad. The key is our response.

> I know what I'm doing. I have it all planned out—plans to take care of you, not abandon you, plans to give you the future you hope for.
>
> Jeremiah 29:11

It is a matter of moment-by-moment living, hand in hand with God. In His perfect timing, He will peel off and transform the layers of our stinkin' onions, challenging us to turn towards Him. It is up to us to approach each part of our day with an adventurous, positive attitude and spirit! It is about substituting our dejected demeanor and complaining words of "I don't know" with standing tall, lifting our arms upward, and positively embracing the words, "I don't know!"

When we refocus on Jesus, expect God's changes, and accept His timing, it is easy to feel like we are on a fast track to His plan for our lives. At this point in our journey, the biggest pitfall, however, is overcoming our pride and learning to become humble. The disciples shared in learning these same lessons. Peter gives us a great example.

> "Simon, stay on your toes. Satan has tried his best to separate all of you from me, like chaff from wheat. Simon, I've prayed for you in particular that you not give in or give out.

When you have come through the time of testing, turn to your companions and give them a fresh start."

*Peter said, "Master, I'm ready for anything with you. I'd go to jail for you. I'd **die** for you!"*

Jesus said, "I'm sorry to have to tell you this, Peter, but before the rooster crows you will have three times denied that you know me."

Luke 22:31-34

And that's what happened within hours: Peter denied Him three times. How can that be? The same way it happens to us. We have good intentions, but then circumstances take an unexpected and/or a difficult turn and we fall back to our "default" behavior, which is grabbing the reins and taking control. However, there is hope if we trust His plan and timing for us. Jesus was not done with Peter, and He is not done with us either.

After breakfast, Jesus said to Simon Peter, "Simon, son of John, do you love me more than these?"

"Yes, Master, you know I love you."

Jesus said, "Feed my lambs."

He then asked a second time, "Simon, son of John, do you love me?"

"Yes, Master, you know I love you."
Jesus said, "Shepherd my sheep."

Then he said it a third time: "Simon, son of John, do you love me?"

Peter was upset that he asked for the third time, "Do you

love me?" so he answered, "Master, you know everything
there is to know. You've got to know that I love you."
Jesus said, "Feed my sheep."

John 21:15-17

Jesus reinstated Peter by humbling him and gracefully giving him new direction. He does the same for us. Without lessons in humility, listening, seeing and behaving become legalistic, churchy routine. Being humble allows us to be compassionate and turns us away from our pride and the judgment of others. Make no mistake, we need eyes to see, ears to hear and a mind to behave in a way that honors God, but without humility, we might as well walk the plank.

⌒ TARA'S JOURNEY

Upon my return from our first Women of Faith Conference, I was renewed like a penny washed in vinegar. I was literally on fire for the Lord, and that feeling oozed out of me. I was better at everything because I was better inside. My relationship with God took on a more vibrant role, and it spilled over into every nook and cranny of my life.

Along with being keenly aware of how my everyday life had been enhanced, I also knew I needed to get to work. I was to use the skills of my past to help others experience this exhilarating type of worship I had encountered at the Women of Faith Conference. It would be a lie to say I didn't immediately fantasize about being on stage at the conference encouraging people on their walk. Fortunately, I was able to discern these thoughts as pyrite.

My "gold" nugget led me to the conference, but it didn't point to my participation in the conference. My gold led me to organizing women in my rural area to experience the event. The magnitude of energy and love for Jesus at the conference was not something that many of us were exposed to in our rural area, and it was life changing! I needed to find a way to make the conference more convenient and more afford-able for my local ladies.

My prequel to motherhood revolved around travel. When my mother, sister and I set out to our first "WOF" Conference with a group organized through a travel agency, my mind was buzzing with logistical questions. Could a bus pick up a group closer to our homes? How do I purchase tickets? Where would we stay? What would make the ladies feel special? How can I save everyone money?

Refining and honing these types of details for our trip was how I spent the next few years. Each year, I organized the two-day, one-night trip. But oddly enough, as soon as we got on the bus, I would tell the group that I wasn't going the following year. Wait, what? Not going, why? My decision not to return did not involve the logistics of the trip. The Lord always took care of selling all the tickets, and over the years our numbers grew to over a hundred people. I thoroughly enjoyed planning the event, and the details fell into place like clockwork. It was prepurchasing the tickets and dealing with purchasing agents that spoiled my experience. The year 2014 was particularly harsh for sales. Sales agents were calling and asking me to book for the 2015 conference, and we hadn't even attended the 2014 conference!

My frustrations followed me for many years. This was my cycle of thinking: plan the trip, get frustrated with the sales process, decide not to go the next year, actually go to the next year's conference, change my mind, start planning again. Year after year, my attendance at the conference brought me out from hiding under my "broom tree" like Elijah (see 1 Kings 19:5-9); I was rejuvenated by the talent and energy of the speakers and the worship. My ticket-purchasing frustrations would be thrown aside, and once again the Lord became my focus. On the drive home from the conference, I'd hop up into the bus and say, "Who's coming with me next year?"

Every year the prepurchase of tickets was a stumbling block for me. I would get very annoyed with the sales tactics, and that annoyance would spill over into my decisions for the overall trip—forgetting that the Lord ensured that I never had unused tickets. The easiest solution was to stop buying tickets and to stop attending the conference. As always, *me, myself and I (MM&I)* started formulating new and better ideas. If the ticket sales were going to make it impossible for my group to attend, then maybe it was time for a change. After all, I was applying my gifts to serve the Lord in this adventure. Did it really matter if I prayed about this decision? I was marching along doing God's work, and I thought I absolutely knew the entirety of His plan. If the business end of this convention was giving us trouble, I vowed to apply my wits to find us a different venue or a different conference. Maybe it was time to hold our own ladies retreat? If it wasn't going to work out for our group to attend this conference, have no fear. I'd be the hero and create a new and wonderful plan for my ladies.

Our 2015 trip brought me two new circumstances that were in opposition to each other. First, I realized I would be returning and bringing a group to the conference each year. The Lord worked hard on me in the off-season. No more wishy-washy nonsense! No more "I don't agree" or "I know better" or "I'm not getting my way, so we won't come next year" declarations. My mission from the Lord was to provide a way for ladies to get to the conference, and I finally accepted it. My opinion on the sales tactics did not matter; I just needed to arrange the trip.

Second, all the tickets needed to be paid in full; the option of making a down payment was taken away. This was a huge financial deal breaker! Part of our trip plan was that I fronted the deposit for the prepurchase of tickets, but I could not afford to pay for the tickets outright. If I could not pay the deposit, there was no way we would be able to secure our box seats.

On the way home that year I tried to contain my anger and frustration with the new payment structure for the tickets. How was I going to plan for the trip the following year? Very few people would be able to pay the full ticket price up front. I remember saying to the group, "Don't worry; we may not all sit together at the conference, but we will be united on our bus and at our hotel." While I was saying that out loud, inside my mind I was making other plans. What if I plan a local event? My gears were shifting, and I started accelerating down a path without God. I rushed full steam ahead with plans for a different event that kept me in control.

Enter the Lord and His lesson in humility. On Monday morning after the conference weekend, I was on the phone with WOF, purchasing a small group of tickets. While waiting for the customer service representative to answer, another call was coming through my line: it was a participant from the bus. I quickly clicked over to her call, hoping to add another ticket to our group order. What I received was nothing short of a miracle. On the other line, I found a beloved sister in Christ. I could hear in her voice that she had more to share with me than just a simple request for a ticket. She had been moved by the Holy Spirit. "Tara, well, we have this money in reserve for emergencies. It is so heavy on my heart that someone may not be able to go next year because we are unable to make deposits. I want you to purchase the fifty-two seats for the bus, and I will pay for them."

As she concluded her Spirit-led offer, we were both in tears. Here, beyond anything I could have hoped for or imagined, was someone willing to pay the total ticket amount for a bus full of ladies. I graciously accepted her offer, and we said our good-byes. I moved forward with my call to WOF and purchased fifty-two tickets totaling $6,760. She was moved by the Holy Spirit to utilize her reserves for the good of many and to help build God's character in me.

"Move out of the way, Tara—out of your own way and out of Mine."

With my head in my hands, I cried, "Lord, I'm sorry. I'm so very sorry for not trusting that You are always in control." Someone else bought everyone's tickets. Someone else is the hero and solved the ticket problem. Someone else was listening and following the Lord's direction. I was *too busy* taking credit for being *the* great trip organizer. I was *too busy* being *the* problem solver. Me, myself and I…(it still hurts to write MM&I so many times).

Because I couldn't come up with a better fiscal solution to pay for the tickets, I almost diverted an entire bus of women away from life-giving, Lord-praising messages. I was wrapped up in my own self-worth and grand ideas. I never gave the situation to God! I was so very consumed with holding up MM&I's ideas that I failed to see that God was nowhere in the equation. I pushed God out.

Through an act of enormous generosity meant for many, one life was greatly changed forever. The Lord peeled off a prideful onion layer from me on that day. He showed me how my confidence in my own abilities was misplaced and how my logic led me onto a path where He was not. He demonstrated how He can do what I cannot imagine. The Lord revealed to me how to be humble. No matter what skills I may possess on this Earth, they are irrelevant without His guidance. His power within us can only surface when we move ourselves out of the way and let Him flourish within us.

> God can do anything, you know — far more than you could ever imagine or guess or request in your wildest dreams! He does it not by pushing us around but by working within us, his Spirit deeply and gently within us.
>
> Ephesians 3:20

We all are subject to these humbling experiences. That is God's way of refocusing our attention on Him. He humbles us out of His great love and refines us so that we can be of service to others.

ROBIN'S JOURNEY

God has brought to me the importance of understanding the moment-by-moment, humbling walk with Him on numerous occasions, but this occasion was life altering. It all happened in the bread aisle of our local grocery store.

DAY 1
As I left work, I got *the* text: "Are you stopping at the grocery store on your way home?" I sighed inwardly, but having conquered the complaining about "everyday stuff" issue, I carefully texted, "What do you need?" "Bread," came the reply.

So, I pulled into the store's lot and quickly found a pull-through parking spot. I vowed to get in and out as fast as I could. I was hungry, tired and ready to get home. I rounded the banana display just inside the entrance and took a left past the diaper aisle and the medicine aisle, turning sharply at the bread aisle.

At the other end of the aisle, I saw someone I recognized, but for the life of me, I could not place the person. Older, wiser people know they should always admit when they can't place a face, but I was neither. Instead, I pretended I did not see the person, grabbed the bread and zoomed through the self-checkout line before I could be stopped by anyone I knew.

DAY 2 – THE NEXT DAY

As I left the office, I got *the* call: "Are you stopping at the grocery store?" *Noooooo*, I groaned in my head. "Why, what do you need?" "Rolls for dinner," came the reply. I am blessed to have a husband who makes dinner, so I try not to complain—but at the end of the day, it is a struggle.

Again, I looked for the pull-through spot and speed-walked to the entrance. I rounded the banana display, took a left past the diaper aisle and the medicine aisle. As I made the turn into the bread aisle, I was thinking about the fact that the rolls were further down in the aisle past the bread. As I glanced up, I saw a person at the very end who I knew.

This was not just any person; this was someone who, through my work, I knew had so many issues that to talk with this individual now would necessitate at least a thirty-minute encounter. I thought about how tired I was and how I didn't want to talk with that person, now, in the supermarket of all places.

With laser focus on the rolls, I did not make any eye contact and scooted to the self-checkout, hoping the person did not see me. However, I got that feeling—you know it—something's not quite right. Some call it "feeling a bit guilty." I call it the nudge of the Holy Spirit. Whatever it's called, I ignored it. My hunger won out, and I zoomed home for dinner.

DAY 3 – THE VERY NEXT DAY

I got *the* call *again*! He needed something at the grocery store! *No way*. What in the world did he need? "Pickles," came the reply. "Pickles for my tartar sauce." *Pickles*! I screamed silently. But the scream died in my throat. I paused uncomfortably and felt a very humbling realization wash over me.

God was sending me to the grocery store three days in a row. All three days, it was at the end of the day, I was tired and I wanted to go home. I did not want to stop at the grocery store. For the past two days, I had seen people I purposely avoided. I was sure that on that day, I was not supposed to ignore the person I would see.

On high alert, I deliberately got into my van and slowly drove towards the grocery store. I prayed for the person I knew I was going to meet and, with anticipation, parked my van in my pull-through spot. I deliberately walked to the entrance, alert and readying myself for an encounter with one of God's children.

I rounded the banana display and walked slowly past the diaper aisle and the medicine aisle. I didn't need bread today; I needed pickles. Where were the pickles?

In the bread aisle, of course!

There she was past the bread, past the rolls, right in front of the pickles. She was an acquaintance who had just lost a family member. I prayed for words to share with her as I walked towards her down the aisle. They were simple words, said compassionately, "How are you doing?" That was all I had to do. We chatted. Nothing earth-shattering happened except, as we parted, she thanked *me* for talking with her because lots of people were just avoiding her. She told me that it was good to openly acknowledge the difficult journey she was on. She had no idea how God used her to teach me a humbling lesson.

I said good-bye knowing that God had peeled off yet another layer and opened my eyes to see once again that there are no coincidences. Being at the right place at the right time is God's timing. We are called to walk in sync with Him moment by moment.

> *"Don't waste your energy striving for perishable food like that. Work for the food that sticks with you, food that nourishes your lasting life, food the Son of Man provides. He and what he does are guaranteed by God the Father to last."...*
>
> *They jumped at that: "Master, give us this bread, now and forever!"*

Jesus said, "I am the Bread of Life. The person who aligns with me hungers no more and thirsts no more, ever. I have told you this explicitly because even though you have seen me in action, you don't really believe me. Every person the Father gives me eventually comes running to me. And once that person is with me, I hold on and don't let go. I came down from heaven not to follow my own whim but to accomplish the will of the One who sent me."

John 6:27, 34-38

When we *refocus* our attention on God and His promises, we give God full control over our lives and ourselves. We *change* according to listening, seeing, behaving and humbling lessons. We learn to *accept* His timing and begin to **flourish** in His love.

To flourish means to cast off any lingering fears and sprint forward in freedom. God gives us *flourishing* life when we abandon ourselves to Him. When we decide to live as He wants us to live, He frees us to see life through His eyes. We receive fruits: love, joy, peace, patience, kindness, goodness, faithfulness, gentleness and self-control. We live in the moment we are in, savoring our relationship with the Father, Son and Holy Spirit. We become one with the God—the Three in One. *God lives where love is.*

Then I heard the sound of massed choirs, the sound of a mighty cataract, the sound of strong thunder:
Hallelujah!
The Master reigns,
our God, the Sovereign-Strong!
Let us celebrate, let us rejoice,
let us give him the glory!

Revelation 19:6-7

VIII

Remember

And that about wraps it up. God is strong, and he wants you strong. So take everything the Master has set out for you, well-made weapons of the best materials. And put them to use so you will be able to stand up to everything the Devil throws your way. This is no afternoon athletic contest that we'll walk away from and forget about in a couple of hours. This is for keeps, a life-or-death fight to the finish

*Be prepared. You're up against far more than you can handle on your own. Take all the help you can get, every weapon God has issued, so that when it's all over but the shouting you'll still be on your feet. Truth, righteousness, peace, faith, and salvation are more than words. Learn how to apply them. You'll need them throughout your life. God's Word is an indispensable **weapon**. In the same way, prayer is essential in this ongoing warfare. Pray hard and long. Pray for your brothers and sisters. Keep your eyes open. Keep each other's spirits up so that no one falls behind or drops out.*

Ephesians 6:10-18

W e need to remember these words not as some lofty ideal but for how they practically guide us through each day. *Remember* is a word that focuses us on the past. It is a word that means stop and contemplate what we already know and sometimes what we have forgotten. God meets us in the moment we are in by reminding us of where we once were. We can't jackhammer out the past. This remembering process helps us look back and recognize what we might not have seen at the particular time of an event. It is a memory refresher for the purpose of compelling us onward in today.

Remember, we can't fully plot the future because we don't know the next coordinate until we enter the new day. We do know our constants—God, Jesus and the Holy Spirit. The only way to prepare for tomorrow is to learn as much as we can from the day we are in through getting to know God. In reality, we will know where we are going once we get there.

God's onion peeling is similar to plotting out where we have been. However, it is where we *are* that our tools are utilized. For instance, loving in the moment is a tool to be used in the face of a difficult situation. We can't love "behind." We need to love in the moment we are in. We have a choice to use our tools and strategies now to follow God or follow self. This was the same choice Adam and Eve had. Remember?

> GOD took the Man and set him down in the Garden of Eden
> to work the ground and keep it in order.
>
> GOD commanded the Man, "You can eat from any tree in the
> garden, except from the Tree-of-Knowledge-of-Good-and-
> Evil. Don't eat from it. The moment you eat from that tree,
> you're dead."
>
> Genesis 2:15-17

Adam and Eve were given a choice. They chose rebellion. The consequence of their choice was death—ultimately separating us from God. Fortunately, it never takes God away from us. He is ever vigilant, wanting us to return. He calls us back to Himself in ways only He understands; each of us is drawn by different circumstances and by different means.

Remember, He has provided us with His love, for that is what He is. He has given us a written "navigation manual" describing the story of His love for us and the depths to which He has gone and will go to bring us to Himself through the journey and self-sacrifice of His Son, Jesus. He has given us a "Navigation Guide," the Holy Spirit, who shows us how to use the navigation tools provided for our journey to weather the storms of this life. Once again, reliance on Scripture and God's promise to us that He will never give us more than we can bear will help us navigate through these unchartered waters without full knowledge but with enough to keep us safe in the freedom of His never-ending love (see 1 Corinthians 10:13).

Remember, our choice is before us. We can give God the control in our lives or we can try to do things on our own. When we finally figure out that reliance on our own efforts does not bring us God's gold but only this world's pyrite, we will want to choose God. When that happens, our lives flourish and become a grand adventure.

Remembering helps us to focus on how to do and how not to do life. The process is sometimes painful, sometimes joyful and many times confusing. Regardless of how we feel in the remembering process with God, we should know that our experiences on our own river journey always have the potential to bring us closer to Him. Hopefully, God has reminded each of us of experiences in our past as we have journeyed through the pages of this book. Those memories point to the places where we have been in order for us to move onward.

Remember...

God *reveals* Himself to us.

God allows us to *recognize* our need for Him.

We *rebel* against God.

God *refocuses* our hearts on Him.

God *rebuilds* the brokenness that threatens to sink us.

God *renews* a right spirit within us.

God *reminds* us to remember Him in every moment.

We *rejoice* in the Lord always.

Each day that God gives to us is necessary to Him. That is why it is so important to remember what we have learned and start our day by staying close to Him. We need God to remind us to look at our map of guiding signposts and to remember where we have stopped along the way so that we can not only avoid those hazards but also help others who are facing similar challenges. At the same time, life is not simply about reviewing the map of past signposts. It also is about looking ahead to where God is guiding us. He has a plan for today that can't be completed if we sit down in our comforts and dwell on the past or fret about the future. Today is our most important day.

ROBIN'S JOURNEY

As I sat with God praying about how I got from my selfish youth to where I am today (point A to point B), I asked God how it is that we are taught these important lessons of life. How are we brought into the life filled with the character of Christ? I was expecting a profound answer. But what God reminded me of was a past event that did not seem profound at all.

It was a cold, wintry day, and I carefully picked my way down the alley trying to avoid icy patches. I shifted my briefcase and the bags I was holding, thankful that I was almost to my office door. However, I should not have had such thoughts because right at that moment, I stepped on a patch of invisible black ice and both my feet went out from under me. It happened so quickly that I did not even have time to register the fall in my mind. I was just suddenly on my back, my head bouncing off the concrete. I lay there for a few minutes thinking thoughts like *I'm glad I'm okay* and *I hope no one saw that.*

Eventually I gathered myself up, retrieved my bags and took the final steps to my office door. As I stood at the door, I realized I had everything but my keys. They had been in my hand when I fell. Where were they? I laid all my bags down and proceeded to retrace my steps; I even looked under the bush near where I had fallen. I found nothing. I proceeded back to my bags, thinking the keys had fallen into one of them. I searched diligently. Nothing.

I returned to the site of the spill and gingerly stood at the exact point of the fall, praying for God to show me where the keys were. And He did; they were right on top of the bush, hiding in plain sight. I thanked Him.

It was an odd event to have retrieved from my memory bank to answer my prayerful question. I pondered the icy fall and my actions. I remembered that I had proceeded carefully, knowing that the way was treacherous. I was carrying my essentials with my eyes wide open, relying on my physical abilities to manage the way. I did not talk to God on the way to my office. In hindsight, I should have been asking Him for sure feet.

However, I was thanking Him immediately after the fall because I was not injured. I know I picked myself up and rejoiced, although with fleeting thoughts about embarrassment. I also know I asked for His help as I searched for my keys, even as I was persistent and careful in my search. I praised Him the whole time, thankful for His help. When I found the keys, I rejoiced!

As I contemplated this reaction, I was reminded of yet another incident that happened five feet away and twenty-plus years before, when I was a baby Christian. Back then, I had parked my van in front of my office one weekend as I traveled with my good friend to visit one of her friends in West Virginia. We stayed at a resort and spoiled ourselves with spa treatments.

I remember sitting in bed at the resort talking to my friend, looking in the desk drawer for the hotel directory, and finding a Gideon's Bible. As I picked it up, I saw that someone had written her favorite Bible verses in the front of the Bible. I remember making disparaging, judgmental comments to my friend about the person who had written the verses, since I considered that to be a desecration of the Bible.

When I came home, my van had a broken rear window. I remember then and to this very day the exact moment when I saw that broken window. I remember because I was immediately convicted and grieved down into my soul. I had made fun of God by making fun of one of His children who had shared her favorite verses from the Bible with me. I had discarded God in that moment because I had treated one of His children with contempt. I repented then.

For many years thereafter, I returned again and again to that incident. I realized that the "armor of God" as set forth in Ephesians 6 provided for protection for us. The armor protects the entirety of our being except our backs; God has our backs. He had my back on that day that my rear window was broken, and He allowed it to shatter to get my attention. Sometimes, in His protection, He allows bad things to happen in order to move us onward.

As I write this today, I think about other "tragedies" in my life. I mean *real* tragedies such as the death of loved ones, house fires, infertility, death of children, the life-threatening illness of my spouse and my parents' terminal illnesses. And yet, the Holy Spirit brought these two relatively innocuous incidents to my mind. Why?

To answer my initial question, of course! How did I get from my selfish youth to where I am today? I am certainly not in any way perfect, but I am much, much further along on the path to right living. *How* did God renew a right spirit within me?

He did it in the day I was in. He did it by reminding me of the circumstances I encountered, watching and encouraging me to react in a way that was worthy of Him. On that day when I fell, I realized that I had not been in communication with Him before the fall as I headed down the alley. I was relying on my own power. That being said, He still was there protecting me from serious injury. What I did do was immediately start conversing with Him and praising Him afterward. Would I have done that twenty-plus years ago? No way!

Many times over the course of my journey, my reactions were not up to His standards, and the Holy Spirit showed me the error of my ways. He did it through choices I was given. Sometimes I failed to make the right choice, and He convicted me of those choices at just the right time. This is why I journal; it is to remember what once was and to look at where I am now. It encourages me and convicts me to do better. It focuses me on what He has called me to do.

Remembering is a holy process between God and each of us. He designs it so we can take the next best steps in our journey today. The process always involves love for us—love brought about by the cross of Christ. Jesus took on Himself all the acts of humankind that separated us from God and laid down His life for us. Jesus, the perfect Son of God, took on our imperfection, dying for humankind as the final and complete sacrifice. By God's grace, this act of selfless love saved each of us. So, lest we forget, Jesus was sent to save us so that we could be reunited with God not only in the future when we die but also in this moment. Since we have been reunited with God through Christ, our future is secure; our past, then, is to be used to remind us of what we should be doing today to gather God's gold for His Kingdom.

Hallelujah!
*You who serve G*OD*, praise G*OD*!*
Just to speak his name is praise!
*Just to remember G*OD *is a blessing—*
now and tomorrow and always.
From east to west, from dawn to dusk,
*keep lifting all your praises to G*OD*!*

Psalm 113:1-3

IX

Rejoice

*Celebrate God all day, every day. I mean, **revel** in him! Make it as clear as you can to all you meet that you're on their side, working with them and not against them. Help them see that the Master is about to arrive. He could show up any minute!*

Don't fret or worry. Instead of worrying, pray. Let petitions and praises shape your worries into prayers, letting God know your concerns. Before you know it, a sense of God's wholeness, everything coming together for good, will come and settle you down. It's wonderful what happens when Christ displaces worry at the center of your life.

Summing it all up, friends, I'd say you'll do best by filling your minds and meditating on things true, noble, reputable, authentic, compelling, gracious—the best, not the worst; the beautiful, not the ugly; things to praise, not things to curse. Put into practice what you learned from me, what you heard and saw and realized. Do that, and God, who makes everything work together, will work you into his most excellent harmonies.

Philippians 4:4-9

The practice of rejoicing is a discipline of life. It is a choice to rejoice in the midst of any situation through turning to Him in worship and praise, reading or listening to His Word, and spending time with Him in prayer. Rejoicing enables us to walk in His will and in His way. Scripture that becomes special to us will leap into our minds as we journey down the river and face the challenges of this world. We can sing praises in the midst of storms, give thanks when our hearts are grieving and fix our eyes on Jesus when we are in impossible situations. But in order to be able to rejoice in tough situations, we must start with the mundane.

⌇ ROBIN'S JOURNEY

I was so sick of the laundry. I mean, it piled up at an ever-increasing rate. The girls were changing outfits for every occasion. The boys were throwing clean clothes into the laundry because I had threatened to ground them if they did not clean their rooms. It always baffled me why they would choose to throw clean clothes in the laundry when they knew I would see them. For goodness' sake, I had just folded the stuff!

That day, as I sorted what seemed like the tenth load of clothes, I got angrier and angrier at the number of socks that were not turned right side out. What was especially annoying was that many of them were my husband's. I remember my mind going off into a deep rabbit hole. At the bottom of that hole, Ted was in charge of a world conspiracy to distribute dirty socks that were inside out. I am telling you that it was not a good day in the laundry room.

In this process, it dawned on me that I was very angry about socks. That truly startled me. It just did not make sense that I would be getting so worked up about socks and laundry. I took a deep breath and thought to myself, *There must be something else that is causing you such angst.* But instead of zeroing in on the "cause," I remembered God's Word in Philippians 4:4 (NIV): "Rejoice in the Lord always. I will say it again: Rejoice!"

That calmed me down instantly. I also should say that I was embarrassed and humbled at the same time. The Lord reminded me of His Word. It caused me to instantly reverse my stinkin' thinkin' because I was nowhere near rejoicing. As I sat in the middle of mounds of clothing, I contemplated His instruction. I did not *feel* like rejoicing. As a matter of fact, I felt like the opposite, but He had specifically told me to rejoice. I made a mental U-turn.

I picked up a sock, Sam's mud-encrusted, inside-out sock, and stared at it. I was compelled to pray and ask the Lord to bless Sam, thankful for the gift of my son and for being his mom. I picked up the next sock, Ted's inside-out, wood-cutting sock with chips of wood embedded in it. As I removed the pieces of wood, I gave thanks for this rugged, wood-cutting man whom the Lord had blessed me with. I asked the Lord to protect him as he cut the wood that we needed to heat our home for the winter. The next sock was Andy's right-side-out, smelly soccer sock. As I lifted him up to the Lord, I noticed that I was smiling—smiling because I was filled with love, joy and thankfulness to God for blessing me with my husband and children; thankful that I had the opportunity to care for them. Praying for my family as I turned their gross socks inside out had given me a new attitude, an attitude of rejoicing.

From that day onward, I lifted up many prayers for my family and my kids' friends who left their socks at our home. I call it my sock prayer ministry. Others may complain about mundane chores like making dinner, going to the grocery store, taking out the trash, walking the dog, paying the bills, changing the toilet paper roll, scrubbing the shower or putting wood in the woodstove. Bottom line is, all these chores are signs of blessings from God of family, food, shelter and everyday life. Our greatest weapon against falling into the trap of complaining is rejoicing.

TARA'S JOURNEY

Although I threw my life at the Lord and told Him to be in charge of it, my reactions to His guidance did not change. Anything in my life that I did not want to do was greeted with the response of "why me?" The Lord's direction of my life made it better in every way, yet I was still a complainer. It was easy to rejoice over major life events like finding my soul mate and having a family. I had the career I always longed for as a stay-at-home mom, and we were financially stable. For these major tangible life benchmarks, it was easy to rejoice and give credit to the Lord.

However, I was not rejoicing in my everyday, moment-by-moment living. I was still stuck in comparing what the Lord was asking me to do with what others apparently were allowed to be doing. For example, if I was gossiping with a friend and later felt convicted, I would ask the Lord, "Why should I be the one who always has to apologize? Why don't You require them to do some changing?" As the Lord spoke to me about my behavior, I always grudgingly complied but still asked the question, "Why me?" His response, in that still, small voice, was always the same: "*Why not you?*"

That question always stopped me in my tracks, but it didn't cause me to rejoice. For me, "*Why not you?*" was the same as the Lord saying, "*Have I not blessed you? Isn't your life better with Me in charge? I died for you, remember?*" I knew the answers to these irrefutable questions. The phrase always made me obey and brought about change, but it did not make me rejoice.

As time moved on, God worked miracles in my life. His blessings quieted my resistance to the changes He wanted to bring about in my thinking and behaviors. The Lord continued to heap blessing upon blessing on this soul to the point that I was frightened. I would say to myself, "God is good, but the world is bad, and there is no way something bad isn't going to happen to me. No one, especially one such as myself, should have the life I live. No one, who has done so many wrong and terrible things, should live this fairy-tale life." I was certain it was only a matter of time before tragedy fell, and it all would come crashing down. I moved from a complaining life to a life of trepidation, yet still not a life of rejoicing.

"Why me, Lord? Please stop. I'm not worthy of all these blessings. You have given me a heart for You, a phenomenal husband, three beautiful, healthy children—please stop. The more You continue to bless me, the more I have to lose."

"*Why not you?*"

"Why not me, what?"

"*Why not bless you?*"

"Wait. What?"

"*Are you not My child, My daughter whom I love? Why not you?*"

All this time of living day in and day out with the Lord, yet it wasn't until that moment that I grasped the true depth of His unconditional love. The God of the universe loves me as His daughter. He sees me as blemish free; He is not keeping a tally of blessings given. My value to Him is priceless.

Believing in and understanding this unconditional love allows me to rejoice in every moment of every day. There is not a limit to what our God will do in our lives if we allow Him to be in total control. Don't hold yourself back. Hand the reins over to Him. He is the Alpha and the Omega, the Beginning and the End, the all-knowing, all-powerful, limitless God who is with us on Earth to show us His love. *Rejoice!*

> *You're blessed when you're at the end of your rope. With less of you there is more of God and his rule.*
>
> *You're blessed when you feel you've lost what is most dear to you. Only then can you be embraced by the One most dear to you.*
>
> *You're blessed when you're content with just who you are — no more, no less. That's the moment you find yourselves proud owners of everything that can't be bought.*
>
> *You're blessed when you've worked up a good appetite for God. He's food and drink in the best meal you'll ever eat. You're blessed when you care. At the moment of being "care-full," you find yourselves cared for.*
>
> *You're blessed when you get your inside world — your mind and heart — put right. Then you can see God in the outside world.*
>
> *You're blessed when you can show people how to cooperate instead of compete or fight. That's when you discover who you really are, and your place in God's family.*
>
> *You're blessed when your commitment to God provokes persecution. The persecution drives you even deeper into*

God's kingdom.

Not only that—count yourselves blessed every time people put you down or throw you out or speak lies about you to discredit me. What it means is that the truth is too close for comfort and they are uncomfortable. You can be glad when that happens—give a cheer, even!—for though they don't like it, I do! And all heaven applauds. And know that you are in good company. My prophets and witnesses have always gotten into this kind of trouble.

Matthew 5:3-12

Jesus went on to tell His disciples, as He looked over the crowds of people, His heart breaking for them because they were so confused and aimless, like sheep with no shepherd, "The harvest is plentiful but the workers are few. Ask the Lord of the harvest, therefore, to send out workers into his harvest field" (Matthew 9:37-38 NIV).

We all are part of God's harvest, and in that knowledge most of us choose to sit down in contentment. Remember in our parable of the river journey, our traveler began in the boat with Jesus, went through trials, chose to follow and submit to Him, and found contentment in being part of His harvest. But in the end, as she walked down the gangway, she realized that there is more than just contentment in a life following Jesus. There is absolute joy, freedom to flourish and always reason to rejoice!

It's our turn to move past contentment and become workers! God has plans for our lives. Wherever He is calling us to serve, let us march forth with this blessing:

The LORD bless you and keep you;
the LORD make his face shine on you and be gracious to you;
the LORD turn his face toward you and give you peace.

Numbers 6:24-26 NIV

X
The Scripture Challenge

Below are the "guiding signposts" we have mentioned as part of our journey. You will have your own guiding signposts. We challenge you to find them.

There are many ways to identify your guiding signposts. However, in the event you would like a suggestion, here is an exercise that might help you. Write a thank-you letter to God thanking Him for getting you from point A to point B. Point A can be any significant date in your life. Point B is a later date. Recognize the specifics of your circumstances at that time. Ask for insight into the situation.

Do you see Jesus when you look back? If not, look again. Are there unresolved aspects to that leg of your journey? If so, talk to Jesus about finding resolution. Then, sit with God and your letter. Ask the Holy Spirit to guide you to a word or a phrase. Take that word or phrase and look it up in your Bible. Trust that the Spirit will take you to the Scripture that speaks to your situation. Write down the Scripture. It is one of your guiding signposts!

OUR GUIDING SIGNPOSTS

Psalm 40:1-3	Reveal	God lifted us out and pulled us up.
Psalm 51:1-6	Reveal	God is generous in love, grace and mercy.
2 Corinthians 5:14-15	Reveal	Resurrection life is through Jesus.
Revelation 3:15-22	Recognize	Buy God's gold.
Psalm 37:5	Recognize	Open up before God; trust Him.
Romans 7:17-25	Rebel	Something has gone wrong deep inside of us.
John 3:16-18	Rebel	God loves us; He sent Jesus so we can have eternal life.
Jonah 4:10-11	Rebel	God's in charge, not us.
1 Kings 18-19	Rebel	Be aware of subtle rebellion.
Hebrews 12:5-11	Rebel	Keep your eyes on Jesus.
Romans 6:20-23	Rebel	Do the next right thing God's way.
Galatians 5:13-17	Refocus	Live a free life God's way.
Galatians 5:19-21	Refocus	Do not live the world's way.
Luke 6:27-49	Refocus	We are stinkin' onions.
Luke 5:1-11	Refocus	Push out into deep water and trust.
Galatians 5:22-26	Refocus	Live God's way; fruits are given.
Jeremiah 29:11	Refocus	God plans good things for us.
Matthew 7:13-14	Refocus	Don't look for shortcuts to God.
Romans 12:1-2	Rebuild	Dedicate the right to yourself to God.
Matthew 6:34	Rebuild	Focus on today; God provides.
2 Timothy 3:15-17	Rebuild	The living Word of God shows us the way.
Matthew 11:28-30	Rebuild	Come to Jesus. Learn to live freely.
Matthew 6:5-6	Rebuild	Pray simply.

1 Corinthians 3:9-17	Rebuild	Build on Jesus. We are the temple of the Holy Spirit.
Psalm 141:3	Rebuild	Guard your tongue.
1 Corinthians 13:6	Rebuild	Love cares for others; it doesn't keep score.
Isaiah 55:8-9	Rebuild	God doesn't think the way we think.
Luke 14:25-33	Rebuild	Jesus must be first in our lives.
John 6:39-40	Rebuild	Jesus puts us together upright and whole, preparing us for eternal life.
Proverbs 2:1-8	Renew	Make insight your priority
Proverbs 15:31-33	Renew	Listen to good advice if you want to live well.
Matthew 6:34	Renew	Keep your entire attention on God.
Jeremiah 29:11	Renew	God has good plans for us.
Luke 22:27-34	Renew	God's not done with us.
John 21:10-19	Renew	His grace restores us.
Ephesians 3:20	Renew	God can do anything.
John 6:27, 34-38	Renew	Jesus sustains us and never lets us go!
Revelation 19:6-7	Renew	The Master reigns—*rejoice*!
Ephesians 6:10-18	Remember	Gear up with God's weapons.
Genesis 2:15-17	Remember	Everyone fails sometimes; turn and obey.
Psalm 113:1-3	Remember	Flourish in service to God.
Philippians 4:4-9	Rejoice	Celebrate God all day, every day.
Matthew 5:3-12	Rejoice	We are blessed!
Matthew 9:35-38	Rejoice	March forth!
Numbers 6:24-26	Rejoice	The Lord's blessing is upon us.